THEORIES OF TECHNICAL CHANGE AND INVESTMENT

Theories of Technical Change and Investment

Riches and Rationality

Chidem Kurdas
Assistant Professor of Economics
Pennsylvania State University

St. Martin's Press

First published in Great Britain 1994 by
THE MACMILLAN PRESS LTD
Houndmills, Basingstoke, Hampshire RG21 2XS
and London
Companies and representatives
throughout the world

A catalogue record for this book is available
from the British Library.

ISBN 0–333–55828–6

Printed in Great Britain by
Antony Rowe Ltd
Chippenham, Wiltshire

First published in the United States of America 1994 by
Scholarly and Reference Division,
ST. MARTIN'S PRESS, INC.,
175 Fifth Avenue,
New York, N.Y. 10010

ISBN 0–312–12181–4

Library of Congress Cataloging-in-Publication Data
Kurdas, Chidem.
Theories of technical change and investment : riches and
rationality / Chidem Kurdas.
p. cm.
Includes bibliographical references and index.
ISBN 0–312–12181–4
1. Saving and investment. 2. Technological innovations—Economic
aspects. 3. Economic development. I. Title.
HB822.K87 1994
338'. 064—dc20   94–5973
                                                      CIP

To my parents
Ayfer and Kemal Kurdas

Contents

Acknowledgments

The evolutionary process that led to this book began with a dissertation at the New School for Social Research. I am indebted to Robert Heilbroner and Edward Nell for their suggestions and encouragement. Richard Nelson provided enlightenment on numerous issues related to technical change. Raymond Majewski helped in myriad ways, and patiently warded off anxiety attacks.

1 Introduction

Like many modern economists, Adam Smith emphasized the role of capital accumulation in the growth of the wealth of nations. In explaining the relative poverty of a particular nation, Smith pointed to the factors that limit investment. For example, commenting on the economic stagnation in eighteenth-century China, he identified such factors.[1] His general diagnosis was as follows:

> China seems to have been long stationary, and had probably long ago acquired that full complement of riches which is consistent with the nature of its laws and institutions. But this complement may be much inferior to what, with other laws and institutions, the nature of its soil, climate, and situation might admit of.
>
> 1776; 1976 edition, vol. I: 111–12.

In particular, Smith argued that Chinese laws and institutions constrain growth by restricting foreign trade.[2] But he also offered another explanation for what he considered to be a case of premature stagnation:

> In a country too, where, though the rich or the owners of large capitals enjoy a great deal of security, the poor or the owners of small capitals enjoy scarce any, but are liable, under the pretense of justice, to be pillaged and plundered at any time by the inferior mandarins, the quantity of stock employed in all the different branches of business transacted within it, can never be equal to what the nature and extent of that business might admit.
>
> Ibid.

Because of the insecurity of small businesses, and the consequent high risk of investment, Smith argues, only investments that promise an extremely high rate of profit are undertaken in China. He implicitly makes an assumption about expectations, namely, that people expect a high incidence of 'pillage and plunder' of small businesses. This expectation, apparently based on past experience, discourages investment.

A typical modern economist would be unlikely to explain this case of secular stagnation any better than or even as fully as Adam Smith did. Any explanation would include the insecurity suffered by businesses as an increased cost of capital. But a large part of the modern literature on

1

growth and investment does not go beyond this point, and offers no insights to add to Smith's story of the mandarins and business people. Could the business people have tried other options in dealing with the extractions of the mandarins, instead of simply accepting the situation as a fact of life? How does their behavior compare to the behavior of businessmen in, say, sixteenth-century Western Europe, where various forms of plunder also existed?[3] Specifically, what makes business people attempt to change such constraints instead of taking them as given?

A quest for a better understanding of what makes for technical and organizational innovativeness versus stasis, for riches versus poverty, brings up such questions about the behavior of economic agents. In their decisions regarding their material life, people are unlikely to be irrational. They behave in accordance with the calculations they make within a certain framework. I will refer to this framework for calculation as the agent's rationality.

1.1   WHAT IS THIS BOOK ABOUT?

What follows is an evaluative survey of various approaches to capital formation, with the goal of clarifying the relationship between investment, growth and technical change. Since these three topics are the subject matter of several enormous literatures, the scope of this survey is necessarily narrow. It may also appear unusual. The focus is on the expectations that underlie investment decisions, in particular on expectations that have to do with technical change. The cost of capital and other financial variables are referred to here only in so far as necessary to describe certain models. The theories are analyzed with a view to understanding how investors' expectations are formed. Financial variables are mostly tangential to the main theme of this book.

The growth accounting literature shows that the contribution of capital formation to the overall growth rate of industrial economies is relatively small, while the 'residual' commonly attributed to technical change is relatively large.[4] But as Abramovitz (1989), among others, has argued, capital formation and technical change are not independent variables. It is the two-way relationship between them (as well as the interactions between other variables) that underlies productivity growth.[5] To understand growth, it is necessary to understand this relationship.

What do we mean by investment? By a broad and general definition, 'Investment is capital formation, the acquisition or creation of resources to be used in production' (Eisner 1987: 980). Probably almost all economists agree that investment is this. But more specific definitions of investment vary. According to the US national income and product accounts prepared by the Bureau of Economic Analysis, gross private investment consists of non-residential structures, producers' durable equipment, residential structures, and change in business inventory.[6] This is a widely used measure of capital formation, but Eisner points out that it is incomplete. The broader definition of investment includes the acquisition of human and intangible capital as well as physical capital, and acquisition of productive resources by government and non-profit agencies, as well as by businesses. Gross domestic capital accumulation in Eisner's alternative 'Total Incomes System of Accounts' is more than three times the magnitude of the more narrowly defined gross private investment in the Bureau of Economic Analysis US national income and product accounts (Eisner 1985: 28, Table B).

The subject of this book is the interaction between investment and technical change, rather than investment *per se*. The kind of accumulation that is directly relevant for this purpose consists of business tangible investment in structures and equipment, and intangible investment in research and development. Residential structures and changes in inventories are beyond the scope of the study. So are investments by public and non-profit organizations, even though such investments can have a significant impact on technical knowledge. These investment decisions have different rationales and, in some cases, are made by agents with other goals. They merit separate explanations. The present survey is confined to private investment that has links to technical change. By rights, accumulation of human capital should be part of the story, but in practice most existing investment and growth models do not deal with human capital, and hence there is little reference to it in the following chapters.

This is a survey of theories rather than empirical studies of investment. Conceptual definitions of capital accumulation, as distinct from empirical measures, are pertinent. Several theoretical literatures have relevance for the subject, and they contain at least two basic distinctions. One is between the flow of investment versus the rate of growth of capital stock. The other is between the Keynesian view of investment as an independent variable versus the neoclassical view of investment as determined by saving.[7] For the purpose of this book, three logically distinct concepts of investment are relevant.[8]

1. In the conventional macroeconomic treatment of the subject presented in macro textbooks, investment is a flow (I) that is subject to short-term fluctuations. What is explained is the absolute magnitude of investment and cyclical fluctuations in this magnitude. The explanation can be along neoclassical or Keynesian lines.

2. In growth theory, the relevant variable is the rate of capital accumula-
    tion, that is, the ratio of investment to capital stock (I/K), rather than
    the absolute amount of investment. In almost all neoclassical growth
    models this ratio is identical to the saving rate. In these models, ex-
    plaining the rate of investment means explaining the saving rate. There
    is no point in making a distinction between the saving and investment
    rates because this distinction brings no gain in explanatory power.
3. By contrast, in Keynesian growth models the rate I/K is defined as a
    variable independent of the savings propensity. That is, the invest-
    ment rate is determined by a different set of forces than those that
    underlie the savings propensity, and requires separate explanation.

Investment and savings can diverge in an open economy. However, a
number of studies show saving and investment in an economy to be highly
correlated with one another, both in a cross section of countries and in
time series (Feldstein and Horioka 1980; Tesar 1991). The distinction between neoclassical and Keynesian growth models is not about the empirical
divergence or equivalence of saving and investment, but about whether
(and to what degree) investment is determined by a set of variables that
are different from those that determine saving. The mechanism that equil-
ibrates investment and saving is what distinguishes the two approaches.

The distinction between the flow of investment (I) versus the rate of
change of capital stock (I/K) is not a matter of dividing the former variable
by capital stock to get the latter variable. The interpretations of the two
variables are different. Distinguishing the rate of change as a variable in
its own right implies that there is a relationship between investment and
capital stock that makes this ratio a meaningful magnitude. The relationship is between investment and the scale of the economy, whether the
latter is measured by capital stock or by national output. It can also be
represented as the share of investment in national product (I/Y). For
example, Adam Smith is clearly concerned with the secular rate of capital
formation in China. It is the ratio of investment to the scale of the economy that is stagnating, not just the annual flow of investment – Smith is
not concerned with temporary fluctuations in the latter. The stagnation he
is explaining is a long-term phenomenon, and his explanation is based on
historical forces that have been in operation for centuries.

Business cycle models tend to focus on the flow of investment, while
studies of growth define capital accumulation as a ratio.[9] Theoretically,
the distinction between the flow of investment and the ratio of investment
to capital stock or output is useful only if there are persistent forces that
underlie the ratio of investment to the scale of the economy. If there are

such forces, it makes sense to distinguish the rate of investment from the absolute amount. Otherwise, the distinction is not helpful in explaining capital accumulation.

Given that this book is about growth and technical change, cyclical variations in the flow of investment are not particularly relevant. However, in surveying the literature, it is on occasion necessary to consider all three definitions of accumulation.[10] For example, in Keynesian models the short-term and long-term concepts of investment are related to one another, and it is not possible to understand one without the other. Unless they have implications for growth, I do not consider models that deal exclusively with variations in the absolute amount of investment. Accelerator models of investment, for instance, are beyond the scope of this book.

If the definition of investment is complicated, the definition of technical change is even more so. 'For technical change is not one thing; it is many things' (Rosenberg 1982: 3). The many forms of technical progress do have a common denominator, namely additional knowledge that makes possible a higher level and/or higher quality of output, for a given amount of resources (ibid.). Schumpeter distinguished invention, innovation and diffusion as the sequential stages of technical change, but there is ample evidence of learning-by-doing and continued innovation during the diffusion of technologies (Rosenberg 1976: 61–84). The strictly sequential view of technical change obscures what goes on, more than it clarifies. Schumpeter emphasized major innovations that represent breaks with existing technologies, while others, such as Jacob Schmookler (1966), focused on series of small, incremental improvements. The different approaches surveyed in this book represent technical change in various ways. I will discuss each of these particular representations in the appropriate chapter.

1.2   WHY DO WE NEED THIS STUDY?

There is not much doubt about the importance of the relationship between investment and technical change for productivity growth and material welfare. The unclear part is what insights economics offers on this subject, why much of what it offers is inadequate, and what can be done about this state of affairs. I have searched for an evaluative survey that helps clarify the issues involved. My search has not been blessed with success. This book is meant to be such a survey.

I asserted above that a typical modern economist would not be able to explain the growth of the wealth of nations any better than, or even perhaps as well as, Adam Smith. From the 1950s to the 1970s a large number of conceptual and empirical studies concerned with the determinants of investment spending were published.[11] From the 1970s on there have been few contributions dealing with this topic. It is doubtful that this relative lack of research on investment is due to the state of perfection achieved by the existing models. Some of the shortcomings of the latter are pointed out in the coming chapters. The relationship between investment and technical change probably received more attention from nineteenth-century economists than twentieth-century economists. Again, this cannot be because the relationship is perfectly understood. In fact, studies on the productivity growth slowdown frequently note economists' lack of understanding, both of this relationship and the slowdown.

It would appear that economics is in something of an impasse with regard to the interrelated issues concerning growth, investment and technical change. A basic premise behind this study is that clarifying the sources of the inadequacies of existing models helps in the construction of a more satisfactory approach. This book is partly about what is wrong with theories of investment and technical change. It is partly an attempt to synthesize a large literature that promises a more substantial understanding of the topic.

1.3   HOW IS THE SUBJECT TREATED?

There is no unified literature on capital accumulation. Different models use one or other of the above three definitions. The long-term and cyclical effects of investment are the subject matter of different literatures that rarely, if ever, overlap. The commonly used investment models are rooted in static macro analysis, where the capital stock is a given. Growth and technical change, if included at all in the model, are exogenous variables. Such models explain investment in terms of the cost of capital with no reference to the dynamic impact of capital formation. Thus the explanation of investment is separated from its role in growth, which is the subject of a different family of models. Furthermore, the micro and macro dimensions of investment are usually studied separately. The macro literature on aggregate investment spending has little to do with the theory of the firm and new studies of the role the firm plays in determining economic outcomes.

The fragmentation is even worse with respect to the interaction between technical change and investment. This topic falls into the jurisdiction of several different branches of economics. Technical change itself, until recently, was primarily in the province of industrial organization. Most growth models took it as exogenously given. Recently growth models with endogenous technical change have become more common, but characteristically do not draw on micro studies of technical change.[12] Besides industrial organization, important contributions to the understanding of technical change and the role of the firm have come from economic history.

Thus the study of the causes and effects of investment has been partitioned between the theory of the firm, macro models, growth models, industrial organization, the economics of technical change, and economic history. Given the degree of specialization in economics, practitioners in these areas do not cross over to other literatures. In the absence of a unified approach, the relationship between investment, growth and technical change has mostly languished in a no man's land.

The present survey cuts across various areas. The juxtaposition of arguments from different fields will hopefully lead to a more coherent understanding of this multifaceted relationship. By showing how the different treatments of investment compare to one another it is possible to understand more clearly the implications, limitations and strengths of various approaches.

Any treatment of investment has to find a way to link the present to the future, since present investment decisions have consequences in the future. A comprehensive explanation of the investment decision has to include the relationship between the causes and effects of investment. As the causes and effects do not occur within the same time frame, this requires a way to string together different periods. Or, to put it in slightly different terms, since a rational investment decision has to take account of the future effects of the decision, a model of capital formation has to specify how decision-makers perceive these future effects.

The specification of how an economic agent takes account of the future depends on how the agent's rationality is defined. The approaches reviewed in this book are based on different views of rationality. Each theory involves an assumption about the nature of the information used in reaching decisions. This assumption, which indicates how economic agents form expectations about the uncertain future, is crucial for the theory's explanation of investment.

For example, in neoclassical models agents face a given set of possible states of the world. Each possible state is clearly defined and complete in all relevant dimensions. Agents are capable of estimating the probability distribution of the possible states of the world. What is not known is which of these states will be the actual state at a future date.[13] Rationality, in these models, is assumed to be the choice of the 'optimum' course of action from a given set of alternatives with given probabilities. Following H. Simon, this view can be described as 'hyper' or 'unbounded' rationality.[14] In contrast, institutionalist/evolutionary explanations assume that there is no given menu, probabilistic or otherwise. Human beings learn about different possibilities, and in the process change their environment. This view emphasizes the limits to our ability to search for, acquire, process and store information. What various views of rationality imply for the relationship between investment and technical change is the main theme of the chapters to come.

What justifies this somewhat unusual perspective on capital accumulation? It is not possible to explain the motives and reasoning behind investment decisions without defining the rational framework in which these decisions are made. Different assumptions about rationality form a typology. This typology is a convenient way to organize the fragmented mass of explanations about or related to investment and technical change. It also provides a revealing way to compare the basic approaches to the subject.

The survey starts with the classical economists who followed Smith, namely Ricardo, Malthus and Marx.[15] I have chosen this starting point because classical arguments foretell the problems that bedevil later treatments of the topic. They provide a backdrop that highlights certain features of later, full-blown, investment and growth models. Chapter 3 shows that the Keynesian conception of expectations leads to a fundamental indeterminacy in post-Keynesian growth models. Chapter 4 attempts to evaluate the variety of neoclassical models that deal with investment and growth. The assumption of unbounded rationality that characterizes neoclassical theory imposes certain requirements on the treatment of technical change in these models. I will argue that these requirements conflict with the observed characteristics of technical change and growth. By contrast, the institutionalist/evolutionary approach focuses on learning and search activities. From this perspective, the behavior of economic agents cannot be understood in terms of optimization. Chapter 5 explains why this is so, and what bounded rationality implies for investment and technical change. The last chapter recapitulates the main points that emerge from the evaluative survey.

2 The Classics: Diverse Behavioral Assumptions

As I indicated in the introduction, this book is about the interaction of investment and technical change. However, the first two sections of this chapter are about investment *per se*. These sections demonstrate how different assumptions about expectations underlie different investment theories. That is their justification.

2.1 MALTHUS VERSUS RICARDO

For classical authors 'accumulation' meant investment in physical capital, and is used in that sense in this chapter. They did not necessarily make the distinction between investment as a flow and as a rate. An early example of different perspectives on investor behavior is to be found in the general glut controversy between Ricardo and Malthus. Ricardo consistently espoused the simple explanation of investment favored by various classical authors:

> The farmer and manufacturer can no more live without profit, than the labourer without wages. Their motive for accumulation will diminish with every diminution of profit, and will cease altogether when their profits are so low as not to afford them an adequate compensation for their trouble, and the risk they must necessarily encounter in employing their capital productively.
>
> (Ricardo 1951, v. 1: 122)

That is, at profit rates that are higher than the minimum necessary to cover the investor's 'trouble and risk', investment is simply proportional to profitability. Below that minimum, investment ceases. From this point of view, all one need do to understand the rate of accumulation in an economy is to consider the rate of profit. As Schumpeter described it;

> the important thing was to have something to invest: the investment itself did not present additional problems either as to promptness – it was *normally* sure to be immediate – or as to direction – it was sure to be guided by investment opportunities equally obvious to all men ...
>
> (Schumpeter 1954: 572. Italics original)

9

Malthus had a more complicated and not as clearly elucidated view of accumulation. According to him, accumulation can be endangered by either the Scylla of too low a savings rate or the Charybdis of too high a savings rate. As a result of the former 'wealth must be gradually destroyed from the want of power to produce', while the latter leads to a situation where 'the motive to accumulate and produce must cease from the want of effectual demand' (Malthus 1836: 6–7). Malthus agrees with Ricardo that investors react to a lower rate of profit by investing less. And, like Ricardo, he forecasts declining profitability for the British economy. Where he diverges is in attributing this fall in the profit rate to a deficiency of aggregate demand, as compared to the country's production possibilities. He believes that the danger of too much saving and a demand constraint is more relevant for the British economy than that of a supply constraint. The relatively slow growth in demand, he asserts, will cause the profit rate to fall, and that, in turn, will result in slower accumulation.

Ricardo, in contrast, predicts declining profitability due to rising food-stuff prices.[1] Referring to the argument put forth by Jean Baptiste Say, Ricardo argues that the rate of profit cannot fall due to a deficiency of demand, 'because demand is only limited by production' (Ricardo 1951, vol. 1: 290). Adam Smith had written that 'the desire of the conveniences and ornaments of building, dress, equipage and household furniture, seems to have no limit' (Ricardo 1951, vol. 1: 293–4). Ricardo points out that Smith is not consistent with his own view when he maintains that accumulation will increase the 'competition of capitals' and thereby reduce the profit rate. Since markets grow at the same rate as capital, there cannot be more 'capital' than 'market', so to speak, no matter how much capital is accumulated. By the same reasoning, Malthus is wrong in thinking that a deficiency of demand can lower the profit rate.

Malthus tries another angle:

You constantly say that it is not a question about motives to produce. Now I have certainly intended to make it almost entirely a question about motives.

(Letter from Malthus; Ricardo 1951, vol. VII: 10–11)

On occasion, both Ricardo and Malthus distinguish the motivation behind investment from the availability of profits to be invested. They separate two aspects of accumulation; the 'power' to accumulate, meaning the availability of funds, versus the 'will' to accumulate. The distinction is not important for Ricardo, because both the 'will' and 'power' are functions of profits and change in the same direction. That is, when profits fall, both the ability to finance investment and the desire to invest are reduced.

However, Malthus inclines towards a possible failure of the 'will' to invest, while for Ricardo the spirit is willing as long as the funds are there. Malthus argues that low expectations of future demand may cause a decline in investment:

> The demand for capital depends, not upon the abundance of present produce, but upon the demand for the future products of capital, or the power of producing something which shall be more in demand than the produce actually employed.
>
> (Letter from Malthus; Ricardo 1951, vol. VI: 117)

So the motive to accumulate depends on the investor's belief that the future output 'shall be more in demand'. Thus Malthus introduces expectations into the picture. With them comes the question that bedevils all subsequent studies of accumulation, namely, what determines expectations? We will come back to this question in the next section.

Malthus explains the relationship between aggregate demand and the profit rate in terms of a specific mechanism. He argues that the level of demand, relative to productive capacity, affects the general price level. Through this effect on the price level it changes the real wage rate, because the money wage is relatively sticky. Hence when there is a strong demand for commodities compared to the amount that can be supplied, prices go up, the real wage down, and profitability improves. Conversely, when demand is weak, workers get a larger share of the product, and profitability declines. This is what causes 'slumps', that is, recessions.[2] It is noteworthy that this relationship between aggregate demand and the profit rate is similar to the 'widow's cruse' idea in Keynes's *Treatise on Money*, and to the relationship between the growth rate and profit rate that is the central focus of post-Keynesian growth models (Pasinetti 1974).[3]

Ricardo and Malthus conduct part of their discussion in the context of the post-Napoleonic War slump. Ricardo does not deny that the end of the war brought economic problems. But he denies that there is an economy-wide slump with lasting ramifications, as Malthus contends. According to Ricardo there is a temporary mismatch between demand and the composition of output, due to the enlargement of sectors catering to wartime demand. The mismatch is in the process of resolving itself, as the overgrown industries shrink and those catering to regular peacetime demand increase employment and output. This adjustment process can have no long-term effect on the rate of profit.

The use of the post-war slump as illustration implies that the controversy is about cyclical fluctuations. But in fact Malthus wants to go beyond an explanation of recession. He argues that low profitability will depress investment not just temporarily but permanently, shifting the economy onto a lower growth path. The recessions are due to demand lagging behind productive capacity, but their long-term impact, in Malthus's view, will be to reduce the growth of productive capacity.

According to Ricardo's reasoning, such an effect can only be temporary. The long-run profit rate is a function of the cost of obtaining sufficient food to keep workers at subsistence level, and it changes only as diminishing returns set in on land, due to accumulation and population growth. Malthus argues that the effects he describes are not temporary.[4] He tries to distinguish 'ordinary' demand and supply from 'accidental' demand and supply (Ricardo 1951: 290). The latter is temporary, he explains, but the 'ordinary' state of demand is a persistent force that accounts for differences in the wealth of nations. He gives examples to show that certain economies, like that of Ireland, are poor because of a lack of demand for their products, while Britain has accumulated substantial productive capacity thanks to its export markets.[5]

Malthus reasons in terms of a succession of actual historical stages. He starts with a high rate of accumulation, such as that experienced in England prior to his own time. Fast-growing export markets have kept demand and profits up for British manufactured products, and as a result investment has been brisk. But this accumulation eventually produces a volume of commodities that cannot be sold at the original price-level on which the investment calculations were based. The larger amount of output can be sold only at a lower price, and this causes the rate of profit to be lower than expected by the investors. At the next stage the motivation to accumulate is weaker, but still with sufficient drive to cause the same situation in the future. This sequential process gradually erodes the secular growth rate.

2.2   AN INTERPRETATION OF MALTHUS'S ARGUMENT

Malthus tries to show that lower capitalist consumption, i.e. more savings, destroys the motivation to invest. He sets up a hypothetical example to show this. 'If the richer portion of society have to forego their accustomed conveniences and luxuries with a view to accumulation', they could invest a larger share of national income to produce 'necessities' for the whole population (*Notes*, Ricardo 1951: 315–16). His example can be expressed as follows:

$$P = L + I$$
$$W = N$$

where P is total profits, L capitalist consumption, i.e. 'luxuries', I investment, W the wage bill, and N worker consumption, i.e. 'necessities'. National income is

$$P + W = L + I + N \qquad (2.1)$$

Malthus reasons, suppose L went down? The additional funds can be shifted to investment. Since the consumption of luxuries has gone down, and since Malthus does not include a sector producing investment goods, the additional investment has to be for the increased production of necessities. Taking the total labor force as constant, there will be a shift of workers from industries that produce luxuries to industries that produce necessities.

Workers can buy these additional consumer goods only if the wage bill is proportionally larger. With the size of the labor force constant, only a real wage increase can provide them with the additional purchasing power. This can come about from a rise in the money wage or a fall in the price level. In either case, the profit rate will be lower. If, on the other hand, there is no redistribution of income from profits to wages, there will be insufficient demand for the additional necessities (N). Without a redistribution of income, equation (2.1) can be satisfied for each period after the reduction in L only if investment remains high. But Malthus argues that investment will not remain at a high level under these circumstances, because investors would not expect it to be profitable.

So by Mathus's reasoning, a drop in L creates a no-win economic situation. If the wage rate goes up, there is demand for the additional goods to be produced, but the profit rate is lower.[6] The lower profit rate discourages investment. Or, the wage rate does not increase and investors perceive that the demand for the additional necessities produced is insufficient. Therefore they cease to invest. It is best, given this framework, to retain a high level of L.

Malthus's hypothetical example makes no sense from Ricardo's point of view. If the affluent citizens are not going to invest, then they would not reduce their consumption, so there could be no issue of demand going down. Ricardo cannot conceive of a failure in both the motivation to invest and to consume. He reasons that if one goes down, the other will go up sufficiently to compensate. In a letter Ricardo expresses this view:

... tho' it appears natural that the desire of accumulation should decrease with an increase in capital and diminished profits, it appears equally probable that consumption will increase in the same ratio... In short I consider the wants and tastes of mankind to be unlimited. We all wish to add to our enjoyments or our power. Consumption adds to our enjoyments – accumulation to our power, and they equally promote demand.

(Ricardo 1951, vol. VI: 135)

Ricardo finds it plausible that generally the desire for both pleasure and power will exceed the capacity to produce. Hence the constraint will be on the supply side. There is no reason for the two motives to add up to less than total income, leading to deficient effective demand. Malthus hints at a failure of motivation on both fronts, but he cannot say why the population should not be as voracious in pursuing 'pleasure' and 'power' as Ricardo supposed it to be. If investors themselves reasoned along the lines that he does, Malthus's argument would be self-fulfilling. In other words, if investors make their decisions on the basis of Malthus's model, they will expect a fall in the rate of profit, and will not invest. If individual capitalists want to save a larger fraction of their income, there is no reason the expectation of generally falling profits should change their mind. If anything, fear of a coming slump may make them more frugal. They may attempt to save at a higher rate, without intending to invest. 'Malthusian rational expectations' of this sort would bring about a recession.

Had Malthus recast the expectation of 'demand for future products' as an independent force, he could have argued that capitalists reduce their investment when they expect demand to lag behind. When they do so, their expectation becomes self-fulfilling. That is, of course, how Keynes argued in the *General Theory*. But Keynes was interested in explaining cyclical movements in output, not secular growth. He argued that investment decisions based on unstable expectations determine employment and national income. As we will see in the next chapter, there are problems in generalizing this Keynesian view of investment to secular growth. Malthus claimed that gluts cause secular decline. A rational reconstruction of his claim requires that individuals continue to save at a higher rate period after period, while not intending to invest. Why such behavior would persist is not clear.

What the Malthus–Ricardo debate shows is how the validity of an argument depends on the use of that argument by economic agents. Investors with 'Malthusian' expectations could bring about a demand constraint. From the Ricardian point of view these expectations are irrational. But if, for whatever reason, investors were persuaded that the Malthusian general glut model explained the economy's workings, and used this model in making decisions, there would be gluts. However, Malthus presented no persuasive reason why expectations might be of this sort.[7]

2.3 MARX'S THREE INVESTMENT MECHANISMS

Malthus's attempts to raise 'a question about motives' made little headway against Ricardo's inexorable logic. Ricardo replied that 'the will is very seldom lacking where the power exists'; the problem was the availability of profits, not the motivation to invest. For Marx, the 'will' is certainly not wanting in the normal run of capitalist growth. But the Marxian accumulation scenario also contains ideas that are related to Malthus's suggestions about a possible lack of motivation. Furthermore, Marx implies that the 'will' to accumulate can increase, possibly leading to a higher growth rate even at the same profit rate.

In effect, Marx has not one but three explanations of investment. These add up to an open-ended story of accumulation. It is open-ended because the profit rate partly depends on the 'rate of exploitation', which is determined elsewhere in Marx's overarching historical scheme. The accumulation story also ties into another part of the overall scenario, namely the argument that increasing capital intensity leads to a secular fall in the rate of profit.[8] For the purpose of this book, only the questions raised by the accumulation story are pertinent. These have some similarity to the issues that continue to bedevil modern treatments of investment spending. The various other pieces of the Marxian scheme are left out of the discussion here.

According to Mark Blaug, the deepest problem in the Marxian system is 'precisely what ... govern(s) the willingness to invest (1985: 254). Blaug reasons that the notion of surplus, central to Marxian economics,[9] depends on the investment question:

> If there is any economic sense in giving the name 'surplus value' to the incomes of capitalists and landlords, it must be because such payments, unlike the wages of workers, are not necessary to call forth the services of capital and land ... The only condition under which the supply price of capital is always zero ... is when neither savings nor investment is in any way connected with the interest rate or the profit rate.
>
> (Blaug 1985: 244)

Therefore in Marx there can be no issue of an inducement to invest. And indeed, Marx indicates that the motivation to invest is not lacking in capitalist society: it is forthcoming in doses large enough to match available profits. But for Marx, the automatic will to invest is a different animal from what it was for Ricardo and what it was to be for later economists.

For other economists, investment is a means to an end, a way of increasing future consumption by giving up current consumption. If Marx's pronouncements are to be taken seriously, he sees investment as an end in itself, as a 'passion'. This is what Blaug refers to as 'conspicuous accumulation for its own sake' (Blaug 1985: 254). Marx sees the accumulation of assets as capitalist society's ultimate criterion of respectability and prestige. Capitalists who do not accumulate lose their status. Marx also attributes the accumulative drive to the quest for power:

> To accumulate, is to conquer the world of social wealth, to increase the mass of human beings exploited by him, and thus to extend both the direct and the indirect sway of the capitalist.[10]

A note elaborates this idea with a quotation from Martin Luther. Marx thus introduces the quote: 'taking the usurer, that old-fashioned but ever renewed specimen of the capitalist for his text, Luther shows very aptly that the love of power is an element in the desire to get rich' (1954, vol. I: 555). Individuals can seek power in different ways, but in capitalist society, Marx believes, a large number of them will seek it through accumulation. In particular, after individuals achieve a certain level of material welfare, further increases in consumption become incidental. Individuals accumulate not because they seek additions to their future consumption, but to acquire more power and status. Translating this behavioral assumption into modern terms, profits above a certain minimum do not correspond to the opportunity cost of capital. These profits are an economic rent.

Also, the economics of the marketplace forces each and every capitalist to strive to expand his capital for fear of being squeezed out by faster-growing rivals. These combined economic and social forces dictate the motto, 'Accumulate, accumulate! That is Moses and the Prophets!' (1954, vol. I: 558). Capitalists are socially conditioned and economically forced to accumulate, and there is a systemic tendency in capitalism to invest whatever surplus is available. Hence Blaug's conclusion that for Marx 'capitalists automatically re-invest all profits regardless of prospective returns' (Blaug 1985: 245). It should be noted that this automatic response allows little discretion on the part of the individual capitalist, who has been conditioned to seek power and status in this particular way.

However, there is still the question of how much will be saved and invested. Capitalists do not invest all profits: part of the surplus becomes 'revenue' and is used for consumption.[11] Marx distinguishes the two uses of surplus value:

> One portion is consumed by the capitalist as revenue, the other is employed as capital, is accumulated....Given the mass of surplus value, then, the larger the one of these parts, the smaller is the other. *Ceteris paribus*, the ratio of these parts determines the magnitude of accumulation.
>
> (1954: 554–5)

The question is how this important ratio is determined. Investment is not a residual left over from capitalist consumption, determined by the capitalist propensity to consume. Investment cannot be a residual if consumption in itself is not the capitalist's goal. On the contrary, consumption is a residual, since the capitalist is motivated by the prospect of augmenting his wealth as an end in itself. In fact Marx asserts that luxury consumption is merely one of the means to protecting one's credit, undertaken in order to assure the world of the capitalist's solvency.

Given the generalized social goad to save and invest and the pressure of competition, there is another explanation for the share of capitalist consumption in profits. Marx states that the propensity to save will adjust if new opportunities for investment arise:

> Under special stimulus to enrichment, such as the opening of new markets, or of new spheres for the outlay of capital in consequence of newly developed social wants, etc., the scale of accumulation may be suddenly extended, merely by a change in the division of the surplus value or surplus product into capital and revenue. (1954: 575)

The word 'merely' in this passage implies that it is easy to adjust the propensity to consume when a 'stimulus' comes along. But the examples he gives of such stimuli involve major changes in the economy. In the *Communist Manifesto*, Marx and Engels had described such changes as responsible for the Industrial Revolution:

> The opening of industry goes on, leading to the rise of modern industry; Meantime the markets kept ever growing, the demand ever rising. Even manufacture no longer sufficed. Thereupon steam and machinery revolutionized industrial production.
>
> (quoted from Tucker 1978: 474)

Presumably the waves of worldwide market expansion continue under advanced industrial capitalism, and present 'special stimulus to enrichment' from time to time. The propensity to save out of profits then adjusts to the increased propensity to invest.

The 'enrichment' here may mean greater absolute profits but not necessarily a higher rate of profit. Marx does not mention the possibility of the latter in describing these situations. It is also possible that the new opportunities encourage expectations of profitability, whether or not the actual rate of return is higher. At any rate, it is possible to interpret the 'special stimulus' so as to avoid the issue raised by Blaug, that the Marxian concept of surplus value would have no meaning if profits were necessary to induce investment.

The 'conspicuous accumulation' and the 'special stimulus' are two different mechanisms of investment spending. The normal operation of the capitalist economy, above the minimum rate of profit necessary for accumulation to take place, is

$$g = s \cdot r \quad \text{for } r > r_{min}$$
$$g = 0 \quad\quad \text{for } r < r_{min}$$

where g is the growth rate of the capital stock, r the profit rate, r_{min} the threshold profit rate below which no investment takes place, and s the propensity to save from profit income.

Marx offers the same explanation as Ricardo for the cessation of investment at rates of return below r_{min}, namely that the risk and trouble of investment is not covered at rates of return below the threshold. The normal operation of the economy is indicated by the schedule $s_1 \cdot r$ in Figure 2.1. When new internal or external markets open up, the savings propensity changes, and the 'normal' relationship shifts, say to $s_2 \cdot r$, corresponding to the higher savings rate. The two types of movement, i.e. along the schedule and shifts on the schedule, are not logically contradictory, but what causes the changes in the savings propensity is not clear.

The 45-degree line in Figure 2.1 indicates the growth rates at zero propensity to consume out of profits. This function

$$g = r$$

sets an upper limit to possible growth paths.

There is yet another aspect to the Marxian investment scenario. This third mechanism is cyclical and based on the temporary divergence of the actual profit rate from the expected rate, as various authors have pointed out (Blaug 1985; Laibman 1983). In his discussion of crises Marx recognizes that the expected rate of profit is part of investors' calculation, and this is a separate factor from the effect profits have in providing the wherewithal for accumulation. The discussion of crises is part of Marx's attempt to show that the profit rate has a tendency to fall in capitalist economies.[12] Marx expects the rate of accumulation to fall with the rate of profit, not only because there are less profits to be invested, but because the motivation to invest is temporarily eroded. To put this into the terms used by Malthus and Ricardo, when the 'power' to accumulate, i.e. profits, fall, the 'will' also diminishes, so that investment falls more than proportionately.

On the face of it, this appears to contradict what has been said before about conspicuous accumulation. Blaug notes that accumulation as Moses and prophets, and accumulation as motivated by the expected rate of profit have different time dimensions. Changes in profitability influence capitalist behavior by disappointing expectations. With a falling rate of return, expectations based on past experience are not borne out and this disrupts accumulation, feeding the crisis. The disruption is temporary. Expectations adjust to the new profit rate and accumulation resumes. Expectations adjust because the underlying need to accumulate overcomes disappointment: 'Once capitalists grow accustomed to a new, lower rate, accumulation resumes, no matter how low the rate may be' (Laibman 1983: 376). Within the Marxian frame of reference, there is no long-term alternative to capital formation: capitalists have to accumulate if they are to remain capitalists.[13]

Obviously, Marx does not imply that capitalists consume more when the rate of profit falls. That does not fit his understanding of what happens in recessions. If capitalists were to switch from investment to consumption there would be no crises due to 'overproduction', i.e. deficiency in aggregate demand. The implication is that capitalists continue to save when their expectations are disappointed and they reduce the rate of investment. In short, Marx sees the profit rate influencing investment not only because profits provide the finance, but because investors expect to make the same rate of profit that they made in the past. The check to accumulation due to the lower rate of profit periodically breeds what Marx calls crises of 'overproduction' and unemployment (Marx 1967, vol. III: 242). These temporary dislocations due to fluctuations in investment, that is, business cycles, are superimposed on the unconstrained social drive to accumulate.

Hence the profit rate does affect the willingness to invest, but only when it changes, and then temporarily. A steady rate of profit does not affect the motivation to invest, i.e. the ratio s, and the economy stays on the $s_1 . r$ schedule (Figure. 2.1). However, Marx expects that the rate of return on investment will tend to fall because of increasing capital intensity, and as this secular tendency shows itself, he expects accumulation to temporarily fluctuate below the $s_1 . r$ schedule.

We now have the three separate elements that constitute Marx's theory of accumulation, summarized in Figure 2. 1.

1. The $s_1 . r$ line shows the 'normal' process, under given circumstances, including the extent of domestic and international market growth, that underlie the savings propensity. It maps a steady rate of profit to a rate of growth of the capital stock.
2. The economy does not move down along the $s_1 . r$ schedule if there is a fall in the rate of profit. It dips below the schedule to the jagged 'crises' area. Capitalists eventually make their way back to $s_1 . r$, at a lower growth rate to match the lower profit rate.
3. When the underlying circumstances change, an increased 'stimulus' to investment causes a shift, for example from $s_1 . r$ up to $s_2 . r$. At the same rate of profit, more is saved and invested.

These three pieces appear to fit together more or less coherently. They constitute a theory of accumulation that in itself is open-ended. Elsewhere

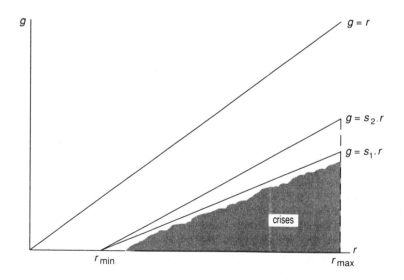

Figure 2.1

in the Marxian system, the power struggle between workers and capitalists determines the rate of 'exploitation' and causes a labor-displacing bias in technical change. These, in turn, determine the rate of profit which can be be plugged into Figure 2.1[14] In the wider context of Marxian analysis, the theory of accumulation may be considered determinate, given the propensity to save.

2.4   THE PATH OF CONSPICUOUS ACCUMULATION

But what exactly creates the 'special stimulus' that causes the shifts in the propensity to save? How do such changes come about? We saw that the establishment of a 'world market' figures predominantly as an incentive for a higher rate of saving and investment in the account of capitalist development given by Marx and Engels. A larger world market provides additional stimulus for accumulation. But what brings about the growth of the market? Marx does not close the three-tiered scenario by adding an exogenous explanation for the shifts. There is little in his writings on this score, and what there is refers back to the capitalists' accumulative drive. 'Modern industry has established the world market', proclaims the *Manifesto* (Tucker 1978: 475). But this suggests that capitalists can pull themselves (and the rest of the world with them) up by the bootstraps: if they invest, modern industry will grow, and the market will expand. The development of the market, in turn, leads to further investment and growth in industry. The 'new markets' and 'newly developed social wants' are then both the cause of accumulation and its effect.

In this light, Marx seems to be describing a secular virtuous cycle, in which accumulation causes market expansion and market expansion causes accumulation. However, this sequence of mutual feedbacks is in danger of collapsing into a pure subjective expectations view of investment. Some post-Keynesians, the subject of the next chapter, subscribe to this view. As expressed by Kaldor, an economy is likely to grow at the rate at which its businessmen expect it to grow (Kaldor 1951). If investors think new markets can be created, and on this basis expand their operations, new markets will come into being.

Is it all a matter of what capitalists happen to expect?[15] Almost certainly, Marx would not have subscribed to this view of accumulation. We will leave the question aside for now, in order to consider the implications of the Marxian growth story.

The capitalist passion to accumulate implies that accumulation in itself enchances capitalists' well-being. Or so Marx's remarks, referred to in the previous section, suggest. If this idea were put into neoclassical terms, the rate of accumulation would be an argument in Marxian capitalists' utility function. Furthermore, Marx distinguishes an early phase of growth when accumulation is the 'ruling passion' (1954 vol. I: 556). Perhaps the marginal utility of an accumulated pound is greater than the marginal utility of a pound spent on consumption. During this phase, shifts from consumption to investment increase capitalist welfare.

Later on in the development of capitalist economies, 'a conventional degree of prodigality, which is also an exhibition of wealth, and consequently a source of credit, becomes a business necessity' (557). If this conventional capitalist living standard is represented by a certain propensity to consume, we get a maximum savings propensity, s_{max}, beyond which capitalists will not be willing to increase accumulation.[16] But increases in the rate of accumulation increase capitalist satisfaction, up till s_{max}.

This leads to a logical conclusion. For Marxian capitalists, the schedule $s_{max} \cdot r$. in Figure 2.2 is the long-run optimum: by saving and investing at s_{max}, they can satisfy their need for accumulation without impinging on their need for the 'conventional' level of luxury. Once at this savings rate, the only way an even higher rate of growth can be achieved is by increasing the rate of exploitation and hence the rate of profit. This is limited by the workers' need for minimum subsistence and leisure. Suppose the latter does not allow a further increase in profits at the expense of

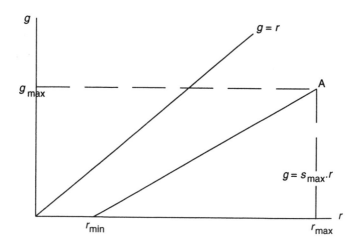

Figure 2.2

workers beyond point (A). Then g_{max} is the highest possible rate of growth of the capital stock that can be achieved, given the capitalist preference for a certain standard of living and workers' preferences for consumption and leisure.

Lacking some external barrier to growth, this is what Marx's capitalists should try to achieve. However, from the way he describes capitalists easily shifting to a higher savings propensity, it appears that they are far from s_{max} at the time he is observing them. What is stopping them from moving to this path of conspicuous accumulation? That is not clear.

Josef Schumpeter thought that Marx's vehement but 'empty' rhetoric against the concept of abstinence was a cover-up. Schumpeter drily commented: 'We need not trouble either Moses or the prophets in order to see capitalists "abstain" with Marx quite as much as they do with Senior' (Schumpeter 1954: 661 n35). The scheme represented in Figure 2.2, partly based on Marx's comments on abstinence, throws some light on this controversy. Until they attain $s_{max} \cdot r$, capitalists cannot be described as abstaining, because they increase their personal satisfaction by saving and investing. Neither can a push up along $s_{max} \cdot r$ be considered abstinence on the part of the capitalists, since this means a reduction of workers' relative consumption. Hence Marx's sarcastic comments on the 'unfortunate' capitalist (1954, vol. I: 557).

On the other hand, the capitalists would be 'sacrificing' if they accumulated at a rate higher than indicated by s_{max}, that is, is they gave up part of the conventional consumption that capitalists aspire to. Rates of accumulation above s_{max} bring 'a Faustian conflict between the passion for accumulation, and the desire for enjoyment'(vol. I: 557). At that point, Schumpeter is justified, in the sense that in Marx's own terms, the capitalists abstain. However, Marx did not consider that to be a real world possibility, since capitalists have the power to decide not to accumulate at a rate that will cut into their desired consumption.

It can be objected that Marx's view of what motivates capitalists is wrong. Probably human nature in general and capitalist human nature in particular is not what Marx thought it was. But that, in a sense, is beside the point. What is interesting about the scenario described here, and what it has in common with later theories of accumulation, is that Marx makes an arbitrary simplifying assumption about capitalist behavior. The implicit assumption is a convenience for Marxian theory, but also a limitation and a weakness.

Consider the possibility of interaction between the three investment mechanisms. Surely, no 'special stimulus' can work during crises. A shift to a higher investment rate must be unlikely when expectations are disappointed. For that matter, how do past profit and growth rates affect the possibility of shifting to a higher growth path? What is the relationship between movements along a savings schedule and shifts of the schedule? Such questions have to do with capitalists' expectations.

In the first two mechanisms described above, namely conspicuous accumulation and cyclically disappointed expectations, Marx implicitly assumes that capitalists behave according to given social rules. This assumption is convenient, because it avoids further questions about what makes capitalists behave in certain ways. Given a savings propensity, i.e. along a $(s \cdot r)$ schedule, capitalists behave like lemmings or programmed robots. They fulfill their social conditioning in normal times and accumulate to the extent that profits allow it. They become disoriented when profits go down, but then resume their programmed accumulation. The point is, they behave automatically, with no discretion.

But the shifts of the $(s_i \cdot r)$ schedule are a different matter altogether. In bringing about such momentous changes, capitalists are behaving not as lemmings but as path-breaking entrepreneurs. There is a gap between the automatic conditioned investor response that Marx assumed in most of his writing and the epoch-changing innovator behavior he mentions on occasion. The two types of behavior may not be inconsistent with one another, but how and why capitalists shift from one mode to another is obscure. How do investors who automatically follow a simple pattern of investment occasionally foresee a 'world market' and break out of their pattern? What makes them stay on a given $(s_i \cdot r)$ ray, and what makes them behave so as to push out the investment opportunities? Since Marx did not pursue such questions about what makes investors behave in certain ways, the shifts remain vague.[17] In effect they are exogenous to the theory.

3 Keynes and the Post-Keynesians: Arbitary Expectations

3.1 CALCULATION VERSUS UNCERTAINTY

Chapters 11 and 12 of the *General Theory* contain two different views of investment. Keynes presented the two chapters as complementary, but others have interpreted them as antithetical:

> Chapter 11 shows us the arithmetic of the marginal efficiency of capital and its relation with interest rates, a matter for actuaries and slide-rules. Chapter 12 reveals the hollowness of all this. The material for the slide-rules is absent, or arbitrary. Investment is an irrational activity, or a non-rational one. Surmise and assumption about what is happening or about to happen are themselves the source of these happenings, men make history in seeking to apprehend it.
>
> (Shackle 1983: 130. First published 1967)[1]

In chapter 11 Keynes takes as given the series of prospective yields from an investment ($Q_1 \ldots Q_n$). The marginal efficiency of capital (MEC) is the discount rate at which the present value of $Q_1 \ldots Q_n$ over the lifetime of the capital asset is equal to its supply price. Within this framework, aggregate investment is determined in a seemingly straightforward way. At the equilibrium level of investment, the marginal efficiency is equal to the current interest rate.

Keynes points out that the MEC would be equal to the current marginal product of capital in a stationary state 'where there is no changing future to influence the present' (1936: 145). But in the real world, the uncertain future impinges on the expected $Q_1 \ldots Q_n$. Orthodox theory, which 'regards the marginal efficiency of capital as setting the pace', Keynes argued, 'assumes that we have a knowledge of the future of a kind quite different from that which we actually possess' (Keynes 1987 *Collected Writings* XVI: 122). Chapter 11 in effect describes what Keynes regarded as the orthodox theory of capital accumulation; then chapter 12 shows that this theory assumes away what matters most in investment decisions, namely our ignorance of the future.[2]

In chapter 12 Keynes describes the effect of stock-market speculation on the long-term expectations that underlie $Q_1 \ldots Q_n$, noting 'the extreme precariousness of the basis of knowledge on which our estimates of prospective yields have to be made' (Keynes 1964: 149). Keynes describes prospective returns as uncertain, and what he means by 'uncertain' is the key to his objection to orthodox theory. Keynes does *not* mean that the probability distribution of possible rates of return is known; he means that there is no knowledge on which to base calculations of marginal efficiency of capital:

> By 'uncertain' knowledge, let me explain, I do not mean merely to distinguish what is known for certain from what is merely probable … The sense in which I am using the term is that in which … the price of copper and the rate of interest twenty years hence, or the obsolescence of a new invention (are uncertain) … About these matters there is no scientific basis on which to form any calculable probability whatever.
>
> (1937, *Collected Writings* XIV : 113–14)

This, of course, is what Frank Knight (1971) meant when he distinguished calculable and therefore insurable risk from uninsurable uncertainty.

In chapter 12 and elsewhere Keynes argues that besides there being no basis for making MEC calculations, there is also less incentive for investors to try to figure out long-term returns in a well-developed stock-market. It is easier to engage in short-term speculation by 'forecasting the psychology of the [stock] market' than it is to forecast prospective yields (1936: 158) What governs investment is not 'cold calculation' of future returns but 'mass psychology', 'conventional valuations' (154), 'animal spirits' (161). Keynes notes that other factors may counter 'the waves of irrational psychology' (1936: 162). But his central message in chapter 12 of the *General Theory* and in his later article (1937) is nevertheless that 'short-period changes in the state of long term expectation' are due to these irrational 'waves'. The combination of these changes and the multiplier give rise to fluctuations in aggregate output and employment, that is, to business cycles.

Thus Keynes objected to his own rendition of the marginalist approach to investment on the grounds that the prospective returns are unknowable and expectations are, to some extent, arbitrary. His particular formula is also logically flawed on another ground, as a number of writers, starting with Hayek, have pointed out.[3] The formula takes the $Q_1 \ldots Q_n$ as independent of the interest rate, so that investment can be determined by a comparison of the latter with the MEC. Given the prospective returns, the effect of a change in the interest rate can be predicted without ambiguity. This yields the inverse relationship, common to neoclassical models, between the demand for investment and the interest rate. But changes in the interest rate generate changes in relative prices and in the prospective returns from capital assets. These changes can be in either direction. For example, because the stream of net returns may decline as a result of price changes, a fall in the interest rate may not lead to an increase in investment spending. A slightly different version of this objection is that changes in aggregate investment spending will affect ex post prices and profitability (Asimakopulos 1971 and 1990).

Keynes briefly mentions a secular concept, the 'normal rate of growth in a given epoch' (1936: 317). He does not explain how the rate of investment that corresponds to this secular growth is determined. He notes that as the characteristics of an 'epoch', notably population growth, change, the average length of the business cycle will also change (318). How exactly these epochal characteristics impinge on the long-term expectations that underlie the expected returns from capital assets is not clear.

In his 1930 essay, 'Economic Possibilities for our Grandchildren', Keynes surmised that cumulative capital accumulation and technical improvements would bring industrial economies to a state of 'economic bliss', where the economic problem of scarcity has been solved. Here, Keynes's view of capital accumulation is not different from Ricardo's. He claims that the savings rate is adequate, and gives no indication that the motivation to invest might be an issue. In 1937, discussing the role of population growth, he explained that the demand for capital depends on the number of consumers, the average level of consumption, and the average period of production (*Collected Writings* XIV: 126). The third factor, a measure of capital intensity, is a function of the interest rate and technical change. The latter appears to be exogenous. His explanation is very much along standard early neoclassical lines.[4]

The 'normal' rate of growth comes into play in Keynes's comments on the earlier version of what later became known as the Harrod-Domar growth model. A key concept in Harrod's model is the warranted rate of growth, (s/v), where s is the propensity to save and v the capital output ratio.[5] The warranted rate is the rate of growth of capital stock that will absorb the savings available each period as output grows. One of the issues raised by Harrod is whether the actual rate of investment (I/K) will be equal to this warranted rate. Keynes agreed with Harrod that in practice the warranted rate of capital accumulation is unlikely to be attained. A burst of capital-intensive inventions and high government expenditure may temporarily push the actual rate of capital accumulation toward the warranted rate, Keynes noted, but 'with a stationary population, peace, and unequal incomes, the warranted rate sets a pace which a private risk-taking economy cannot normally reach and can never maintain' (1938; *Collected Writings* XIV: 349–50). The normal rate of accumulation, then, is not equal to the warranted rate determined by the savings propensity: I/K diverges from s/v.

This implies that the secular rate of investment is independent of the rate of savings, just as the absolute level of investment in a given period is determined independently of savings in Keynes's short-run theory. Harrod's growth model raised the issue of what determines the secular rate of investment. It appears that in coming to terms with Harrod's dynamic analysis of the relationship between investment and savings, Keynes moved away from the Ricardian/early neoclassical view of capital accumulation he had used in his previous discussions of secular growth. He moved towards a view more consistent with his explanation of business cycles. However, he provided no new explanation of the secular rate of investment. What he wrote about unstable expectations is about deviations from a possible long-term trend, not about the trend rate itself.

In summary, Keynes argued that the information necessary to calculate the MEC is usually lacking and that long-term expectations, and hence investment, are subject to arbitrary fluctuations. Furthermore, there is a logical problem in the MEC concept. Keynes seems to have also thought in terms of a secular rate of investment on occasion, but what little he wrote on this normal rate of accumulation is either no different from what neoclassical economists of the time thought, or is too vague to constitute an alternative explanation.

Starting from this basis, Keynesian economists went in three different directions in their treatment of investment. The common 'neoclassical synthesis' response was to ignore the logical flaw and confine Keynesian macroeconomics to the short run. The MEC formula, and the inverse relationship between investment demand and the interest rate, became staples of textbook macroeconomics. The swings in mass psychology, etc. could be accommodated as deviations from a long-run general equilibrium, deviations that did not have to be explained any further, since the model was concerned with only short-term fluctuations in output and employment, and for this purpose took the state of expectations as given. The second path was to forget the MEC and the schism between chapters 11 and 12 of the *General Theory*, and explain investment purely as an optimization problem. The logical inconsistency of the MEC concept and the disturbing implications of chapter 12 made this neoclassical option an attractive one. The problems of ignorance and irrational expectations simply disappeared in the neoclassical world of fully specified production functions and marginal productivity conditions. Since this approach is the subject of the next chapter, I will not pursue it here.

The rest of this chapter is about the third direction, which was the one espoused by post-Keynesians. This group of researchers on the one hand took chapter 12 of the *General Theory* seriously, and on the other, attempted to generalize the short-run reasoning to secular growth. These attempts took the form of equilibrium models at a very high level of abstraction, with uncertainty embodied in arbitrary expectations. The suggestions Keynes made in chapter 12, for example that when knowledge is lacking decisions are often based on conventions, could not be developed within these models. We will see that the arbitrary expectations simply made these growth models indeterminate, without leading to a better understanding of investment decisions and technical change.

3.2   THE INDETERMINACY OF ROBINSON'S GROWTH MODEL

Joan Robinson was one of the leading post-Keynesian growth theorists.[6] With respect to investment, she subscribed to Keynes's position in chapter 12 (and the 1937 *Quarterly Journal* article) that information on future returns is lacking and expectations are partially irrational. In her interpretation, this meant that economic reasoning about investors' expectations is not possible. Trying to find the expected rate of return that underlies investment decisions is like looking in a dark room for a black cat that probably is not there (Robinson 1965: 192). Only a 'comparative historical anthropology' can throw light on the rate of capital accumulation, but we can study the proximate causes and the consequences (Robinson 1965: 55–6). Since Robinson did not provide an explanation, it is unclear what she meant by a 'comparative historical anthropology'. It is clear, however, that such a study cannot be attempted within the highly abstract macro framework she and other growth theorists used.[7]

Robinson's growth model was meant as a generalization of Keynes' *General Theory*. Unlike neoclassical models where investment and savings are determined simultaneously, Keynesian models treat investment decisions as separate from and logically prior to the determination of the level of savings in an economy (Pasinetti 1974: 42–8). This independence of investment from savings is the main distinguishing characteristic of the Keynesian approach, since it is this independence that allows for the demand-side determination of output and employment.[8] This characteristic gives rise to two separate questions, namely the determinants of investment and the relationship between it and savings.

Kaldor suggested that the 'Keynesian technique' of independent investment decisions 'could be alternatively applied to a determination of the relation between prices and wages, if the level of output is taken as given, or to the determination of the level of employment, if distribution (i.e. the relation between prices and wages) is taken as given' (Kaldor 1970: 81–2). Kaldor defended this double use of investment on the grounds that the level of employment and output is a short-run variable, while the distribution of income between wages and profits is a stable, long-run variable. The absolute amount of investment determines the level of output in the static Keynesian model where the capital stock is assumed to be given, while the rate of increase of the capital stock determines (within limits) income distribution in the post-Keynesian growth models.

The post-Keynesian distribution mechanism, commonly called the 'widow's cruse' after an expression used by Keynes in the *Treatise on Money*, is an answer to the question posed by Harrod's growth model.[9] What keeps the rates of investment and saving in equilibrium as the capital stock and aggregate output expand? In Harrod's terms, what makes the actual rate of investment, I/K, equal to the rate 'warranted' by the savings propensity and the capital output ratio, s/v?

Consider a two-class, two-sector, closed pure market economy in which all wage income is consumed and a fraction of profit income is saved.[10] The relationship between the rate of increase of the capital stock and the savings propensity can be re-written as

$$r = I/s.K = g/s \qquad (3.1)$$

where r is the rate of profit and g the rate of capital accumulation. Suppose there is a rise in g. How is the equality re-established? In the post-Keynesian growth story, the increase of investment and consequently aggregate demand, assuming that output is given, puts upward pressure on prices. There is another assumption here, namely that the money wage rate is sticky compared to the price level. Hence when prices rise, the real wage rate falls, and the profit rate rises.[11] Thus equation (3.1) is interpreted as representing a relationship between the rate of capital accumulation and the secular distribution of income between wages and profits.[12]

There are two relationships at the core of Robinson's growth model. One is equation (3.1) and the widow's cruse story, according to which the rate of capital accumulation determines the rate of profit. The other is the investment function, according to which the rate of profit determines the rate of accumulation. Robinson argued that no existing theory of investment, including Keynes's MEC schedule, is capable of explaining the rate of accumulation in the economy as a whole. The latter depends on the 'historical, political and psychological characteristics of an economy' (Robinson 1964: 37). These, it seems, are beyond economic theory. But she has to give some account of investment to complete the model, which she does:

> It seems reasonably plausible, however, to say that, given the general characteristics of an economy, to sustain a higher rate of accumulation requires a higher level of profits, both because it offers more favorable odds in the gamble and because it makes finance more readily available. For the purposes of our model, therefore, the 'animal spirits' of the firms can be expressed in terms of a function relating the desired rate of growth of the stock of productive capital to the expected level of profits.
> (Robinson 1964: 37–8)

In practice, Robinson makes the rate of capital accumulation a function of the realized rate of profit. Hence her explanation of investment closely resembles the classical view of investment exemplified by David Ricardo, with Keynes's 'animal spirits' thrown in to emphasize the instability of expectations. But Robinson does not explain the relationship between expectations and the actual rate of profit.

Figure 3.1 is Robinson's representation of these two relationships. The investment schedule (*I*) shows the rate of capital accumulation as a function of the rate of profit; the distributional relationship (*A*) shows the rate of profit as a function of capital accumulation. Between them they determine the rate of capital accumulation (*g*) at which the profit rate that governs investment decisions is equal to the profit rate that results from these decisions. This is the 'desired' rate of accumulation.

Given the way Robinson drew the investment function *I*, there are two desired accumulation rates in Figure 3. 1. The rate at *D* is stable, the one at *S* is not. When the realized profit is higher than the profit rate that informed investment decisions, i.e. the *A* schedule is above the *I* schedule, investment plans are revised upward. Thus, above *S*, the economy grows faster and faster until it reaches point *D*. Conversely, when the investment function is above the *A* schedule, accumulation shows down. So accumulation rates above *D* are temporary. If the economy were to settle at *D*, there would be a stable and steady rate of accumulation and a matching profit rate.

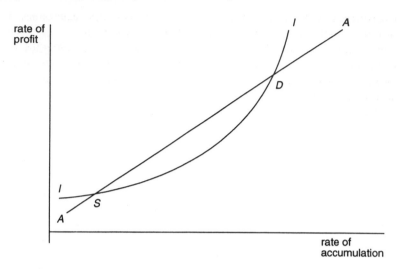

Figure 3.1

The rest of Robinson's growth story is about the various barriers to achieving this configuration and about how the desired rate of accumulation interacts with other variables. These other variables, namely technological change, the growth rate of the labor force, the availability of natural resources, the initial capital stock and the bargaining power of workers versus capitalists, make certain profit and accumulation rates impracticable. Thus a desirable rate of accumulation may not be feasible or it may cause social problems such as growing unemployment. In particular, by comparing the rate of growth of the labor force and the factor using bias of technical change with the desired rate, Robinson defines alternative growth paths that she calls 'ages'. Since her typology of growth paths has little bearing on the central theme of this chapter, I will not discuss it any further.[13]

Robinson's entire approach to growth, including the definition of alternative growth paths, is based on the determination of the desired rate of investment. But the *I* schedule that determines this rate is the weakest link of the story. The position and functional form of the schedule are arbitrary. The only conceptual basis for the schedule is the 'plausibility' of investment as a positive function of the rate of profit. This is too weak to justify a positive slope at all values of the rate of profit; it is more plausible that the slope is generally non-negative, and positive for some values. Robinson herself acknowledged that the assumed shape of the investment function is arbitrary; there is no logical or empirical necessity for it to have the shape depicted in Figure 3.1 (1964: 49, n.1).

Instead, the investment function can be as shown in Figures 3.2 and 3.3. In Figure 3.2 there is an indefinite number of desired rates of growth, in Figure 3. 3 there is none. The outcome depends entirely on how one draws the investment function, and since there is no rationale for any particular configuration, the growth model is indeterminate.

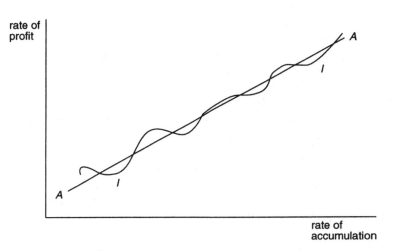

Figure 3.2

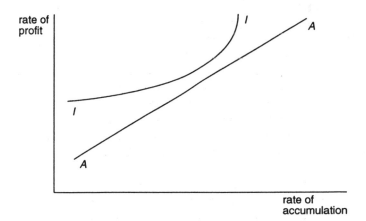

Figure 3.3

The logical structure of this growth model is similar to that of the multiplier accelerator model (Samuelson 1969). In the Cambridge growth model accumulation determines the profit rate, which governs the rate of accumulation. In the multiplier accelerator model investment determines aggregate output, which drives investment. The structural similarity is not surprising, in view of the common Keynesian root of the two models. The similarity also shows in the indeterminateness of the models.

Multiplier accelerator models were used by some authors to analyse cyclical fluctuations (e.g. Hansen 1964), by other authors to explain steady growth (Duesenberry 1958). Pasinetti (1974) points out that the same structure generates either cycles or steady growth, depending on the parameters assigned to the investment function. Consequently the model cannot be used to explain both cycles and growth. Whether one gets growth or contraction or cycles depends on the arbitrary paramaters: 'although the various authors have implicitly shown well-defined preferences for some particular values of the parameters of the investment function, they have not developed any explicit discussion to justify their positions' (Pasinetti 1974: 67). Robinson's post-Keynesian growth model has the same indeterminacy, in that its outcome depends entirely on the arbitrary shape and position of the investment function. Little can be said about the existence, uniqueness and stability of the desired rate of accumulation without justifying the particular function, but there is no explanation in the literature to this effect.

The Keynesian treatment of investment poses another, perhaps more serious, problem for the analysis of growth. There is no explanation of how expectations evolve in secular time, and the link between the actual rate of profit and investment decisions goes through 'animal spirits'. That is, the post-Keynesian approach to expectations remains confined to Keynes's discussion of short-term fluctuations in long-term expectations. Given its dependence on chapter 12 of the *General Theory*, the investment function is unstable. It can fluctuate with any change in mass psychology. Of course, every time the investment function shifts, the desired rate of accumulation (or the configuration of possible desired rates) changes. There is nothing in the model to give the rate of accumulation even a minimal degree of persistence. And according to the post-Keynesian model, with every shift in the desired rate of accumulation, the distribution of income changes.

Keynes's proposition that free-floating business expectations cause fluctuations in employment and output rests on the observed cyclical character of these variables. It has not been recognized that extending the Keynesian argument of volatile expectations and investment to long-term growth leads to inconsistency. In contrast to employment and output, the distribution of income between wages and profits is not subject to cyclical fluctuations; it changes very slowly over decades. Furthermore, stable income shares was a 'stylized fact' accepted by the Cambridge growth theorists. How an unstable rate of accumulation determines a stable income distribution is a question not addressed by Robinson.

Recently the distributional mechanism at the center of post-Keynesian growth models has been questioned on another ground. The critics argue that there is no reason for changes in investment demand to cause permanent changes in the distribution of income between wages and profits (Garegnani 1992; Ciccone 1986; Vianello 1985). Firms in capitalist economies routinely carry sufficient excess capacity to accomodate fluctuations in the level of investment. So output adjusts to changes in capital accumulation, and there is no pressure on income distribution. In this view, even if a rise in investment is too large to be accommodated by increased capacity utilization and supply bottlenecks develop, any fall in the real wage and rise in the profit rate will be temporary. Hence investment in particular and autonomous demand in general affect only the level of aggregate product, not income distribution.

This critique has an implication for the way capital accumulation is viewed.[14] As already noted, the profit rate and profit share are secular variables representing the long-term distribution of income in the post-Keynesian growth models.[15] Changes in this distribution require long-term economic, social, and political adjustments. For example, a rise in the share of profits (and a corresponding fall in the share of wages) entails a traverse of structural change. Given the assumption of differential savings propensities from wages and profits, the shift in income distribution towards profits implies a change in the average propensity to consume. This requires a change in the sectoral allocation of both the capital stock and the labor force, with the industries that produce capital goods growing and those that produce consumer goods shrinking. Furthermore, the attitudes, customs and conventions that embody the living standards of different social groups have to adjust to the change in income distribution, to make it acceptable to the majority of the population. All of these adjustments require time. If income distribution is the way an economy adjusts to a higher rate of accumulation as Cambridge growth theory indicates, the change in the rate of profit and in income shares has to be long term. That is, it has to be persistent enough that the sectoral composition of the economy and social expectations adjust to it.

The relationship between accumulation and distribution implies that the rate of accumulation has the same time dimension as income distribution. If there is no long-run rate of accumulation, there is no justification for the relationship, given that income distribution is a long-run variable. In short, if there is no persistent rate of capital accumulation, then there is no relationship between accumulation and income shares. If investment is a purely cyclical variable, the critics of the post-Keynesian growth model are justified in arguing that fluctuations in investment are connected to employment and output, but not to distribution, that there is no long-run counterpart to the short-run Keynesian demand-side model.

The distinction between the flow of investment and the ratio of investment to capital stock or aggregate output is relevant here. The validity of the link between capital accumulation and income shares depends on there being a persistent, meaningful ratio of accumulation.[16] The absolute level of investment is a highly volatile variable that, put together with the multiplier, explains business cycles. Changes in this variable are not persistent, and cannot be linked to the distribution of income. The latter is a relatively stable configuration that changes infrequently and slowly. Cyclical fluctuations in investment have a different time dimension from secular shifts in distribution. The distributional effect is plausible only if there is a similarly stable and slow-changing rate of accumulation.

Robinson claims that the widow's cruse mechanism works even if 'the rate of investment is not tethered by a particular ratio to the value of the capital stock' (1980: 22). As just explained, this is not the case. She does mention a 'long-run average growth'. Growth may occur in cycles around an average which itself remains steady 'for a run of years' (1980: 23). This is possibly similar to what Keynes described as the epochal 'normal' rate of growth, but Robinson does not make the connection. At any rate, the idea remains unsubstantiated, only a vague possibility that may or may not exist.

Does the share of investment in aggregate output have a significance apart from the absolute level of investment? Is investment 'tethered by a particular ratio to the value of capital stock'? In other words, is there a long-term rate of accumulation? We will consider the answers provided to this question by other post-Keynesians. It is useful to remember that Robinson thought the rate of accumulation is determined by historical and institutional circumstances. It must be these circumstances that do or do not give rise to a persistent rate of accumulation. But these circumstances are beyond the abstract equilibrium growth models.

3.3 KALECKI: A DUAL TIME STRUCTURE

In a sense Kalecki is a forerunner rather than a follower of Keynes.[17] He independently analysed the relationship between aggregate demand and resource utilization and reached conclusions similar to Keynes, but with more emphasis on the link between aggregate demand and profits. Unlike Robinson, Kalecki was careful in distinguishing the different time-dimensions of investment spending. Perhaps the most interesting aspect of Kalecki's work on investment is its attempted integration of the secular trend with cyclical variations.

Kalecki elaborated the business cycle version of the widow's cruse mechanism, based on variations in resource utilization rather than the secular distribution of income. His analysis of the business cycle in general, however, is beyond the scope of this book. The following summary isolates his comments on investment, without going into the explanation of cycles that is the context of these comments.[18]

Kalecki formulated his basic ideas regarding investment in several different ways over the years. Towards the end of these attempts he noted that his earlier versions of the investment function were not entirely satisfactory, in particular because 'By this separation of short-period and long-run influences I missed certain repercussions of technical change which affect the dynamic process as a whole' (1971: 166).

The following equation is a summary of Kalecki's various formulations.[19]

$$I_{t+\theta} = A(T) K_t + B(T) \cdot [S_t; \Delta p_t / \Delta t; -\Delta K_t / \Delta t]$$

The dependent variable here is aggregate investment, and the explanatory variables are economy-wide aggregates or averages. The time subscript 't' denotes variables subject to cyclical changes, while 'T' shows the effect of secular factors that underlie the parameters of the equation. $B(T)$ is the function that measures business responsiveness to what Kalecki sees as the main cyclical influences on the investment decision, namely firms' internal savings (S_t), changes in profits ($\Delta p_t/\Delta t$), and the rate of increase in the capital stock ($-\Delta K_t/\Delta t$), which has a negative effect on investment. These cyclical variables affect investment with a time lag of θ.

Kalecki placed some weight on retained earnings (S_t) both as the direct means of finance and as the indicator of firms' ability to raise funds from outside. Clearly this is a version of the classical theory of investment, modified slightly to fit the modern firm better. He considered changes in profits the main determinant of the expected rate of return, without providing an explanation of how expectations are formed. Note that p_t is the absolute amount of profits. Barring recessions, one would expect it to increase with the scale of the economy. Capital formation leads to greater profits and the latter lead to more accumulation. The negative impact of the rate of increase of the capital stock is similar to the effect of the capital stock adjustment version of the accelerator, but Kalecki does not explicitly consider the relationship between this variable and the rate of change of output. The latter has an impact indirectly through profits and retained earnings.

The function that governs the response of investors to the cyclical variables in the square brackets, $B(T)$, itself changes in the long run, but is stable in the short period as investment fluctuates with retained earnings, changes in profits, and the rate of change of the capital stock. $A(T)$ shows the effect of secular forces that do not work through the cyclical variables. The parameters $A(T)$ and $B(T)$ evolve over time, but the changes in them take longer stretches of time than the changes in the variables in the square brackets. Thus the Kaleckian investment function has a dual time structure, with the coefficients $A(T)$ and $B(T)$ changing in secular time, but acting as constants in the shorter time span of cyclical fluctuations.

The slow-moving 'development factors' Kalecki represents with $A(T)$ include innovation, social and political shifts, and population growth. If there is a secular trend rate of change of capital stock, obviously $A(T)$ is a main component of it. Kalecki says little about innovation, except that innovations give rise to additional investment (1969: 158–9). Again, no explanation is provided of this effect, or the possible reverse effect of investment giving rise to innovations. The rate of innovation is implicitly treated as exogenous, as are the other components of $A(T)$ such as population growth.

Kalecki is known for the methodological proposition that 'the long-run trend is but a slowly changing component of a chain of short-period situations; it has no independent entity' (1971: 165).[20] Going by this statement, $A(T)$ and $B(T)$ may be thought as interacting with the cyclical variables. Possibly Kalecki was thinking of such interaction when he asserted that the scope of the development factors increased with the extent of the capital stock (1971: 151). Later versions of his investment function incorporate the capital stock as an explanation of trend rate of investment. The level of the capital stock determines the rate of investment necessary to embody the given number of innovations. However, it is not clear why innovations should be of this particular embodied type. In spite of these efforts by Kalecki, the secular factors in general and innovation in particular remain exogenous in his treatment.

It may be that technical change appears exogenous in this framework because the framework is simply incomplete. In conclusion to his last attempt on the subject of investment, Kalecki writes:

> To my mind future inquiry into the problems of growth should be directed not towards doing without such semi-autonomous magnitudes as A(T) and B(T) but rather toward treating also the coeficients used in the equations ... as slowly changing variables rooted in the past development of the system.
>
> (Kalecki 1971:183)

Clearly, Kalecki's attempt to use the capital stock to link investment in one period to investment in later periods is inadequate for this purpose. Neither does this treatment provide novel insights into the relationship between technical change and investment. Nevertheless, it sets a research agenda for explaining the trend rate of capital accumulation. Contrary to Kalecki's remark that the long run is only a chain of short runs, explaining the secular parameters of the investment function requires going beyond the cyclical variables. The function is indeterminate in the same way Marx's r–g schedule is, since the interactions and feedbacks that cause the shifts are not clear.

In short, Kalecki pursues the interesting idea that cyclical and secular variations in capital accumulation can be integrated in one function. However, the function does not go much beyond a shopping list of different components. To become a comprehensive and coherent explanation, the listing of possible variables has to be supplemented with a discussion of the interactions between them, and with the secular factors that appear to be endogenous in the function. Kalecki's formulation shows what is missing, but does not fill the gaps. He himself was not satisfied with his own, or for that matter anybody else's, analysis of investment, which he called 'the central *pièce de résistance* of economics' (1971: 165).

3.4   THE TECHNICAL PROGRESS FUNCTION

Kalecki took one step further than Robinson in distinguishing the cyclical and secular effects on investment. Kaldor went further still than Kalecki in explaining the secular rate of capital accumulation.[21]

To understand Kaldor's treatment of investment and technical change, it is useful to refer to the critique he and Robinson directed against the conventional production function view of technology. Kaldor and

Robinson questioned the distinction between a change in capital intensity and a change in technology, arguing that a change in capital per worker almost always entails some kind of innovation (Kaldor 1957: 595). For this reason, it is not possible to distinguish between movements along the production function and shifts of the function. Indeed, the very existence of a production function is in question. Alternative techniques with different capital intensities do not exist as fully specified blueprints, but have to be developed. Recent research provides some vindication for this view.[22] For example, in summarizing a large empirical literature Nelson and Winter conclude that 'almost any nontrivial change in product or process, if there has been no prior experience, is an innovation' (1977: 48).

Instead of the production function, Kaldor proposes a 'technical progress function'.[23] He suggests that productivity growth is a function of accumulation:

$$y^* = a + bk^*$$

where y^* and k^* are the growth rates of per worker output and capital input, respectively. This is a macro relationship. The model does not address the Keynesian issue of the equality between savings and investment and its dynamic Harrod version of maintaining the equality as capital stock grows. Instead, investment is simply assumed to be equal to savings and output is assumed to be at full capacity utilization along the growth path.[24]

The exact functional form this idea takes has changed over time with the different versions of the model.[25] Kaldor describes technical progress as being subject to diminishing returns to capital accumulation. Graphed, it looks like a conventional production function except that it has a positive intercept (Kaldor 1961: 208, Fig. 16). I will stay with the the linear expression for convenience. The main points and the following evaluation are not affected by differences in the specification of the function.

As Kaldor explains it, the coefficients a and b represent the degree of 'inventiveness' in the economy and the willingness of economic agents to adopt new ideas and methods. The technological progress function involves a given level of technological dynamism in the economy:

The postulate of the existence of a given curve presumes, of course, a constant flow in the rate of new ideas over time. Variations in the flow of new ideas, and in the readiness with which they are adapted, are likely to be reflected in shifting the height of the curve...

(Kaldor 1957: 596)

There is an implicit assumption here that technical change is embodied in capital equipment. Given a regular flow of invention, the technical progress function shows the impact of investment on the embodiment and therefore diffusion of these innovations. Kaldor argues that a high rate of investment means fast diffusion and therefore high productivity growth (1957: 595–7). In his account of technical change, investment does not affect 'the rate of new ideas over time'; the latter is exogenously given.

Kaldor defines long-term equilibrium as a constant capital to output ratio. The equilibrium condition is therefore

$$k^* = y^*$$

Given this condition, the technical progress function solves for a unique equilibrium growth rate:

$$k^* = y^* = a/1-b$$

Thus the equilibrium rate of growth of the capital stock ($a/1-b$) is determined by the technical progress function alone, independently of the other relationships in the model. Savings and investment adjust to bring about this growth rate.

Kaldor assumed that there is a 'desired' capital/output ratio at a given rate of profit to which the economy will tend along the growth path defined by the equilibrium condition. He justifies his definition of dynamic equilibrium as follows:

> The assumption that for each enterprise there is some *desired* amount of invested capital in relation to turnover which is itself a rising function of the rate of profit can be justified by the greater risk and uncertainty of expectations for the more distant future as against the nearer future ... A high capital/output ratio implies a longer period of commitment because it implies a higher ratio of fixed to circulating capital.
>
> (Kaldor 1957: 600, n1, italics original)

Investment is undertaken to bring about the desired capital/output ratio. Since the latter is a function of the profit rate, the proportion of income invested is a positive function of changes in the profit rate. We have seen that classical economists thought investment spending is governed by profits. Kaldor is very close to Ricardo in this respect.

Given a profit rate, the desired ratio is fixed and rate of investment is such as to bring the ratio to the desired level. When the economy is not in steady state, the investment function is:

$$k^* = y^* + fr^*$$

where r^* is the rate of change of the profit rate. This function determines the rate of investment along the traverse that takes the economy toward the steady-state growth rate of $(a/1-b)$. The steady-state growth rate itself depends only on the technical progress function and the long-run equilibrium condition.[26] At the equilibrium rate of growth, the rate of profit is constant, so that $r^* = 0$.

The plausibility of this framework depends partially on the plausibility of the premise of an exogenously determined and relatively stable technological 'dynamism', to use Kaldor's somewhat vague expression. This is what underlies the parameters a and b of the technological progress function, and these parameters determine the equilibrium rate of capital accumulation and productivity growth. The steady rate of growth determined by these two parameters is exogenous. In a sense Kaldor merely pushed back one step the question of what determines technical change. He made it dependent on given parameters representing an exogenous technological 'dynamism'.

We saw that the relationship between investment and the profit rate, as analyzed by Marx, Robinson and Kalecki, has an element of indeterminacy. In Marx and Kalecki's growth models the factors that underlie the functions, and cause shifts, are endogenous but unexplained. In Robinson's the factors are exogenous, but too volatile to account for the long-term rate of capital accumulation. Kaldor sidesteps this problem. He achieves the closure of his growth model by assuming that these factors are given and sufficiently stable.

This assumption is curious in view of his criticism, described above, of the conventional production function. Kaldor argued that techniques do not exist as ready-made blueprints and should not be represented as such. A change in capital intensity requires learning and developing the technique to be used, and this is not usefully shown by given parameters. Yet the technological progress function rests on the assumption that technical change exists as a blueprint, with given parameters. Otherwise, movements along the function can change the rate of innovation that is taken as given in constructing the function. The function is in effect a production function of new technologies. It can be defined only if the *production of new technologies* is immune to learning by doing and by using. In view of Kaldor's objection to the production function as implausible, this seems even more implausible.

In fact, the linear approximation of the technical progress function can be integrated into a regular production function, which turns out to be identical to Cobb-Douglas (except in one respect: Hahn and Matthews

1964). The function can also be derived from a vintage capital model that explicitly rules out learning.

Kaldor's technical progress function is not useful in understanding learning effects in technical change. If a higher rate of capital accumulation brings new knowledge about innovation or diffusion, the reversibility of the function becomes problematical. If there is learning and the function is reversible, then there must be unlearning as well, and that is highly inplausible. If, on the other hand, the function is irreversible, the economy's initial rate of accumulation becomes of paramount importance in determining whether a steady-state rate of growth can be achieved and what it will be. But the model has no way of dealing with such path dependency, and nothing to say about the learning process and irreversibilities.

If techniques have to be developed, then the way of changing techniques has to be developed too. Why should the way technology develops be given exogenously? What exactly is the technological 'dynamism' that is supposedly independent of capital accumulation? Kaldor has no answers to these and other questions. At any rate, he himself appears to have been dissatisfied with the technical progress function. Later in his career this dissatisfaction led him to less abstract studies of growth, focused on specific industries and countries.[27]

Nevertheless, this treatment of endogenous technical change was an early harbinger of things to come, not in the post-Keynesian approach but in neoclassical theory. The treatment of technical change in the more recent new classical growth models is in some respects similar to Kaldor's model. The new models too make productivity growth endogenous and determine a steady state growth rate based on exogenously given parameters. The limitations of Kaldor's technological progress function also prefigure those of the new classical models. These are the subject of the next chapter.[28]

3.5 MARK-UP PRICING AND INVESTMENT PLANS

We saw that in post-Keynesian growth theory the distribution of income between wages and profits is a function of the rate of capital accumulation. This is a macro relationship. Post-Keynesian models of firm pricing decisions include a micro relationship between the mark-up and the firm's investment plans.[29] These oligopoly models suggest that profits at the firm level are a function of investment decisions.

The type of firm relevant for this approach is the modern corporation run by career managers who plan the long-term growth of the enterprise, that is, the 'managerial firm' (Marris 1964). Much of the managerial firm literature of the 1960s and 70s developed independently from the business history literature.[30] But the corporation postulated in the managerial mark-up models is the same phenomenon as the corporation whose development has been chronicled in detail by Alfred Chandler (1977, 1990). This is a large multi-unit firm that is likely to be horizontally and vertically integrated. For example, there may be backward integration to control raw material supplies and forward integration to coordinate marketing with production.

The large modern corporation internalizes functions that the single-function, single-unit firm transacts with outsiders. This is the main point documented by Chandler's historical research and the basic assumption of managerial firm models. For functions such as securing materials, marketing, finance, or personnel training, the multi-unit corporation is more likely to substitute in-house administrative coordination for market transactions with outside agents. Chandler argues that this internalization of some functions follows from the scale and scope of the enterprise, and in turn makes possible economies of scale and scope.[31] The internalization economizes on transaction costs that would be incurred in dealing with outside agents.[32]

The mark-up models in the managerial approach to the firm rest on the argument that investment in plant and equipment is one of the functions that is partially internalized. Not only are these activities subject to long-term planning, but the funds to be used for these purposes are primarily generated internally.[33] That is, the finance of future projects is not left to outside agents in money markets, but partly kept under the control of the corporate management, which borrows only a fraction of the investment funds required. To make sure that the requisite funds will be there, pricing decisions are coordinated with long-term investment plans.

A possible explanation of this reliance on internal funds for investment is the transaction costs of borrowing. Depending on the financial institutions, the marginal transaction cost of borrowing, whether by issuing new stock or bonds, may be greater than the marginal benefit of relying on external finance.[34] However, the explanations offered by mark-up theorists are not explicitly in terms of transaction costs. For example, Wood (1975) argues that significant reliance on bank loans is undesirable from the management's point of view because of the borrower's risk it involves, in addition to the risk of a high debt to asset ratio. Futhermore, there are a number of deterrents to new stock issues, according to Wood.

The main disadvantage is the downward pressure exerted on share prices by the increased supply of shares, which inflict a capital loss on existing shareholders. New stock issues may also threaten the incumbent management's position by making take-overs easier (Nell 1992a). There may be principal versus agent issues arising from a divergence of interest between managers and stockholders, but these are not systematically investigated in the mark-up literature.

In these models internal finance of investment is achieved by setting the mark-up so as to provide funding for the corporation's long term investment plans. The latter are not the same thing as actual investment spending. In this scenario, there are two distinct decisions, one to undertake a certain amount of investment at a future date and the other to put into practice a planned project in the current period (Nell 1988). Different considerations come to play in these long- and short-term decisions. It is assumed that the long-term plan is based on the expected secular growth rate of the firm's market, while immediate spending on investment is a function of current sales. The mark-up is determined by the former.

The implication is that investment plans are relatively stable, even though investment spending is cyclically volatile.[35] The investment plan is a tool the management uses to protect the firm's position in the market (Marris and Wood 1971). In order to protect the firm's market share, productive capacity is planned to grow at least as fast as market demand. Otherwise, the firm is at risk of not being able to satisfy future demand, opening the way to new entrants and/or expansion of existing competitors. To reduce this risk, planned investment is geared to the expected secular rate of market growth, which by its nature is relatively immune to cyclical fluctuations. The mark-up, and therefore corporate profits, are a function of the secular expected rate of growth of market demand, and as stable as this trend rate. Thus this type of mark-up model may provide a way out of the impasse that afflicts the distributional mechanism of the post-Keynesian growth model.[36]

This is some of the reasoning to be found in the literature that centers around the link between an oligopolistic firm's demand for investment and the 'plus' over average cost. In these models the corporation marks up average cost so as to generate the funds necessary to finance the investment plan. The plan does not vary cyclically, and neither does the mark-up. This micro explanation of corporate profits then forms the foundation for the macro relationship, with the aggregate profit share determined by the summation of firm investment plans. The mark-up models provide a tentative explanation for the observed relative stability of the profit share.

The distinction between the investment plan and investment spending also provides for flexibility in the latter. The plan is made under uncertainty. An unanticipated experience after the plan was drawn brings doubts as to the timing of capacity creation, leading to a slow-down or speed-up in investment spending. For example, faced with an unexpected fall in sales, management may try to hedge its bets for the time being by slowing down investment spending, yet keep intact the long-run plan geared to secular market expansion. Assuming that the plan is based on an estimate that proves correct *ex post*, there is nevertheless the possibility of fluctuations due to doubts about timing in the process of putting the investment project into practice. The fluctuations in spending around the planned trend rate of accumulation fit into the Keynesian explanation of business cycles. These fluctuations can be explained, for example, by an accelerator type relationship.[37]

From the point of view of the growth of the firm, the pricing decision has two effects. One, it influences the future growth of sales, and two, it provides the retained earnings to finance the growth of capacity. The growth-focused mark-up models are developed around these two relationships. I will describe each relationship in turn.

The dynamic effect of the price of a product on the growth rate of demand for that product, in contrast to the static relationship between price and the absolute level of demand, is a relatively unexplored topic.[38] Various authors in the literature under review simply assume that the dynamic relationship is similar to the static one.[39] The usual list of variables are subsumed under the *ceteris paribus* assumption in order to isolate the effect of price on market growth. Thus consumer preferences, incomes, prices of related products, and expectations regarding future prices and income are assumed constant. Constant macro variables include income distribution, population and prevalent lifestyles. Changes in these variables and the emergence of previously non-existent substitutes and complements cause shifts in the relationship between price and market growth.

A standard consideration with respect to the price elasticity of demand is how narrowly the product is defined. Obviously, the narrower the focus, the greater the price elasticity of demand. When the unit under consideration is the industry, the question is to what extent potential substitutes are included in the definition of the industry. It is possible to make the definition so inclusive that there is little possibility for substitution and the price elasticity is accordingly low. As noted below, the issue of price elasticity becomes particularly complicated when the macro implications of price changes are the issue. For the sake of exposition, I will initially assume (as most mark-up models do) that the growth of demand is relatively price elastic and that the market growth rate is correctly forecast by firms. Since the expected and actual rates coincide, the market growth schedule represents both *ex ante* and *ex post* growth rates.

The second relationship is between the price and the rate of capital formation. Per unit price can be expressed as

$$p = VC(1 + M)$$

where VC is variable cost and M the percentage mark-up.[40] The mark-up is a function of fixed cost, including interest payments and (arguably) dividends, as well as the firm's estimated future need for internal finance. A certain minimum dividend may be a fixed cost from the management's point of view, because the failure to pay it may endanger the top management's position. External finance has a negative impact on M. In short, the mark-up can be shown as a positive function of the planned rate of capital formation (g) and fixed cost (FC) and a negative function of external borrowing (B):

$$M = m(g; FC; B)$$

On the basis of this explanation of the mark-up, the relationship between price and capital formation is an upward sloping schedule that shifts when the components of fixed cost or the conditions of external finance change.

In short, at the level of the firm, the growth of market demand is a negative function of price, while capital formation is positively related to price. Leaving for later the discussion of the premises behind this model and accepting the arguments at face value for the moment, the two functions determine a price that provides the investment funds consistent with the market growth expected at that price. To go from the oligopolistic firm to the industry brings up the question of the reaction functions of firms. Most mark-up models assume that the oligopoly is a price leader, but alternative assumptions of oligopolistic strategic competition have been suggested.[41] Further, economy-wide aggregation raises other issues, some of which are discussed below. Ignoring these aggregation problems, the long-run investment plans translate into a more or less stable profit share, depending on the stability of the variables that underlie the two functions.

The analysis can be developed in terms of shifts of the schedules (Figure 3.4). When the parameters of the market growth (D) and capital formation (S) functions change, the firm changes the investment plan. The shifts can be a result of firm behaviour. For example, if the firm can

increase the growth rate of sales by advertising, both schedules shift
simultaneously. Arguably, advertising is subject to diminishing returns, so
that (D) shifts out by progressively smaller increments (Nell 1992a).
(S) also shifts up due to the increased fixed cost. These shifts trace out a
locus of growth rates and prices (and corresponding mark-ups), each pair
involving a different investment plan. If it is assumed that the corporate
bureaucracy finds it in its interest to maximize the growth rate of the
enterprise, as for example Marris (1964) argued, then this model determines a long-term growth rate. g^*, at which advertising expenditures are at
an optimal level (Figure 3.4).

The different versions of the investment-based-pricing model are
generally based on partial equilibrium reasoning, in the sense that the
aggregate parameters of the (D) and (S) schedules are taken as given. For
example, both schedules are predicated on a given money wage rate.
When the analysis is generalized to the economy, some of these exogenous variables necessarily become endogenous. Simply adding up
industries to arrive at a macro version of the model is in fact a fallacy of
aggregation. As Wood pointed out, the schedules have a clear interpretation in the Marshallian setting, but become problematical if they are
taken to represent macro relations (1975: 106–11).

One particular complication introduced by aggregation has to do with
investment plans. In mark-up models investment plans are geared to the
expected growth rate of the market, which is partly a function of the

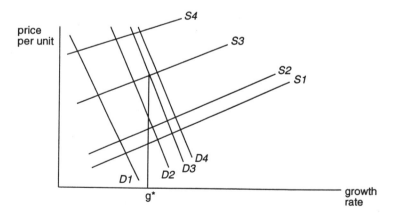

Figure 3.4

growth rate of national output. This is relatively straightforward insofar as the dependency is one way; that is, as long as the growth of national output is independent of business estimates of it. Business expectations can then be seen as based on an objective phenomenon, in the sense that there is an independent variable, the trend rate of growth of national output, and firms project it into the future. For the single firm or perhaps even single industry, an exogenously given growth rate of output may be plausible. But outside the safe haven of partial equilibrium, the growth rate of output is affected by firm's investment plans.[42] That is, the expectations of growth influence the rate of growth of potential output.[43] Because of this interdependence, the mark-up models, like the post-Keynesian growth models discussed previously, imply that the economy grows at whatever rate managers expect it to grow, as Kaldor explicitly maintained (1951). Post-Keynesian models do not explain expectations: unexplained expectations feed on themselves. There is no independent basis for the expectations underlying investment plans; they are arbitrary, in the sense that they are presumed to be inexplicable. The growth models, like the static Keynesian output model, assume expectations are arbitrary. Expectations cannot be explained and have to be taken as exogenously given. But unlike the static model, the growth and mark-up models implicitly assume that expectations are relatively stable. What makes arbitrary expectations relatively stable? We are back in square one, facing Joan Robinson's problem.

Putting this matter aside, the mark-up models imply a solution to the Harrod problem of gearing the growth of investment to the growth of savings, that is, the actual growth rate to the warranted growth rate (Eichner 1976; Wood 1972; Nell 1989b). This problem is internalized and solved by firms, since they link investment to the mark-up (and hence retained earnings). Firms decide what the trend rate of capital formation (I/K) is going to be and determine the warranted rate (s/v) accordingly. In the secular time horizon the economy grows at that rate, although in the short-run there may be divergences from the planned path. If, for whatever reason, managers come to expect a different market growth rate, they invest at that rate and they create corporate savings at that rate, in the long run. Whatever rate of growth they expect is 'warranted', since corporate savings are adjusted to it, that is, I/K is equal to s/v for all I/K. As Wood concludes, 'the aggregate share of investment can be whatever the corporations wish it to be, because this desire for investment at the same time determines the share and rate of profit' (1971: 59).

The mark-up model and the conclusion that the corporation internalizes the warranted rate problem raises a number of questions. Perhaps the simplest objection is that corporate enterprises constitute only part of the whole economy. The corporate structure has competitive advantage in some industries, as Chandler has shown. But in other industries, in particular in parts of agriculture and services, it has no such advantage, and consequently has not developed. Therefore, even if one accepts the mark-up argument, it is not clear that the firm level link between investment plan and price is so prevalent in the economy as to lead to the equalization of economy-wide capital formation and profits. Eichner argues that the non-corporate sector is so small that the corporate economy effectively dominates capital formation and profits. The relative importance of different types of business is an empirical question that cannot be pursued here. Most of the works cited in this section do not address it.

The models assume that the corporation correctly estimates the future growth of demand. The investment plan and the price of the product are based on this correct estimate. This is plausible for a given product with an established market as long as no new complements or substitutes appear. Hence, the applicability of the basic mark-up model is limited to mature industries in a state of steady growth (Eichner 1976: 24, 89). Both new markets, where the growth of demand is unpredictable, and declining markets are excluded from the analysis (Nell 1989b). The relevant setting for investment-based mark-up pricing is the middle of the product life-cycle, a time when technical change is incremental and future of the industry within the firm's planning horizon is predictable. Perhaps the stereotypical example of this type of industry is automobile manufacturing in the US until the late 1960s.

The problem is, the mark-up model is valid under conditions which are not in keeping with the characteristics of the institution that justifies the model in the first place. The modern corporation is an agent of innovation that typically initiates and moves through many product cycles. It is 'an effectively diversified enterprise [which] attempted to have a number of product lines, each at a different stage of the product cycle' (Chandler 1977: 479). Such an enterprise does a balancing act between different products and uses revenues from older product lines to finance the launching of new lines. This is how corporations stay competitive. But these institutional features are awkward for the mark-up model. The relationship between investment and price is most clearly defined for a single product subject to predictable market growth. It requires additional assumptions and becomes cumbersome when adapted to the real-world corporation of multiple products and different product cycle stages.

We have looked at Kaldor's theory of technical change. Other post-Keynesian authors have also tried to explain endogenous technical change (Eichner 1991, chapter 5; Milberg and Elmslie 1992: 111–14). Nevertheless, within the mark-up models innovation is not a central question. Indeed it is something of an inconvenience, since it opens up the Pandora's box of how exactly the corporation estimates its future investment needs. In contrast to the post-Keynesian view of oligopoly which works best in a tranquil world where pricing decisions are based on a known or at least achievable growth rate, consider the Schumpeterian view of the oligopolistic firm. For Schumpeter, innovation is the reason the corporation has competitive advantage over other types of firms, at least in some industries. The oligopolistic structure itself is geared to continual technical change and is a necessary ingredient in this process. Barriers to entry, excess capacity used for defense of market share or for aggression, price rigidity – Schumpeter argues that these practices help the corporation 'gain the time and space for further developments'. Firms do not change their prices when demand goes down, because demand is price-inelastic at such times and lower prices would only hamper the firms' long-term innovation efforts (Schumpeter 1950: 87–106). Recent arguments that the transaction costs of contracting out R&D or acquiring new processes and products from outside agents are relatively high in some industries fit in with the Schumpeterian vision. These high transaction costs explain why these industries are dominated by multi-unit oligopolies with in-house R&D facilities (Teece 1988).

It would seem that any theory based on the existence of the modern corporation as institutional datum has to take into account the fact that typically the corporation spans both mature and new products.[44] Models that apply only to established products throw little light on the behavior of the modern corporation. Since managers have to consider different product cycles and the requirements for successful innovation in their investment plans, the theory needs to explain how pricing and investment decisions relate to the entire range of products.

Acknowledging that the corporation's ability to use profits from one product to finance investment in another product gives it an advantage, Eichner proposes the following way of tying prices of individual commodities to an overarching investment plan.[45] He suggests a criterion for allocating the corporate investment fund among industries: the firm will equalize the discounted rates of return from different products (1976: 118). Obviously, if the return is higher in one industry compared to another, the firm can improve its overall profitability by allocating more investment to the first and less to the other. A new venture is undertaken if the discounted rate of return is higher than that from existing products.

This sounds familiar and simple. It sounds familiar because it is nothing but a restatement of the MEC formula. It sounds simple because it abstracts from the questions Keynes raised in chapter 12 of the *General Theory*. And, if the formula is generalized to the economy, the discounted rates of return cannot be considered exogenously given, as the firms' investment decisions determine the rate of profit. As was the case in the Marxian model, if the firms invest, they bring about a higher rate of growth for the economy. In the mark-up approach, they also bring about the profit share to finance that level of investment. But what makes them invest in the first place? And what makes them invest in one potential new product but not another, when they have no informational basis for estimating the rate of return of either product? These questions remain outside the scope of the mark-up model.

Putting these objections aside and continuing with the post-Keynesian argument, it is possible to add together the firm's planned investments in various products, and to derive a multi-product market growth schedule. With this market growth schedule and a multi-product capacity growth function, an average mark-up can be determined. Any change in the product mix causes a shift of these functions. The exercise is not particularly useful for understanding capital accumulation and technical change, since aggregation across products obscures the rationale for investing in any particular one. Levine (1981) and Shapiro (1981) suggest integrating the product cycle with mark-up pricing, but do not discuss the specific mechanism regulating investment in this framework. Canterbery (1992) proposes an evolutionary simulation model of technical change with mark-up pricing, but that goes beyond this chapter's subject matter.[46]

Products that have a regular and predictable life-cycle can perhaps be included in the post-Keynesian approach. The corporation can be thought of as internalizing the product life-cycle just as it partially internalizes investment finance. Suppose managers know that the growth of a product will follow the pattern of slow start-off, acceleration, slow down, and they know when the turning-points will occur in the growth rate of demand. They plan investments in the product accordingly.

During the early part of the life-cycle, the firm tries to improve the new product and to persuade consumers to accept it. The producer learns how to produce the product more efficiently, how to make it more attractive, how to market it better. This is a process of learning by doing (Arrow 1962) and learning by selling (Thomson 1986, 1987) that includes improvements in product design as well as process innovation and increased productivity. Due to developing consumer taste for the product, the market demand schedule shifts to the right. Due to the increase in productivity, the capital formation schedule also shifts to the right. The net effect on the price and the mark-up depends, of course, on the parameters of the schedules and the relative magnitudes of the shifts. If managers expect market growth to accelerate as per unit cost falls, they will set the profit margin accordingly to finance a higher rate of capital formation.[47]

At some point, the potential for further expanding the market is exhausted, and accelerated capital formation comes to an end. The schedules become stable, and the price is adjusted to a steady rate of planned investment. In some cases, the mark-up on the product may become a function of the firm's investment plans in other products once accelerated growth in demand for the product ceases, that is, once that market becomes a mature one. The proceeds from the product are then used to finance R&D and physical capital formation in other products. The mark-up and thus the price of the initial product may become independent of the market for that product if it seems to have little further potential for growth and the corporation's long-term plan is concentrated on other markets. The capital formation function (*ss'*) for a 'cash cow' product is flat, because the mark-up and price are determined by factors outside the market for this product (Figure 3.5).

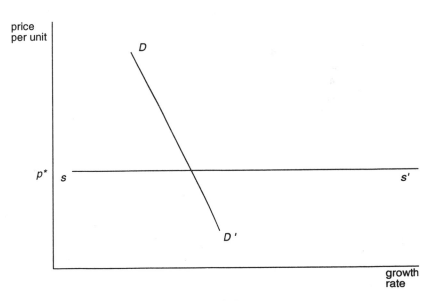

Figure 3.5

This is an implication of the Schumpeterian view of the corporation as an agent of ongoing innovation and competition in the race to introduce new techniques. The mark-up models do not specify the conditions under which the link between capacity creation in a product on the one hand, and the mark-up and price of that product on the other, weakens or disappears, as the firm prepares to abandon the mature market.

The introduction of a successful new substitute, whether by the same corporation or another firm, may signal the end of the life-cycle of the initial product. The market growth schedule then shifts to the left, and the rate of capital formation falls (Figure 3.6). The growth rate may become negative. If the earnings from the product are being used to develop and launch new products, the price may remain fixed at p^*.

All of these developments are possibilities, but there is no basis for a more definite scenario of what happens along the product life-cycle or for understanding what kind of life-cycle different products are subject to. It is also not possible to say much about how product growth paths generalize to the multi-product corporation. And mark-up models offer no satisfactory answer to a crucial question, namely, what difference all this makes for the economy at large, where at any one time there will be products at different stages of the life-cycle.

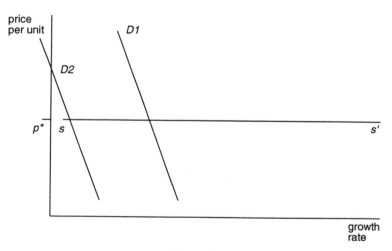

Figure 3.6

3.6 A KEYNESIAN–CLASSICAL HYBRID

An intriguing recent synthesis of the post-Keynesian perspective with classical ideas on investment spending is due primarily to Stephen Marglin.[48] This attempt starts from the empirical observation that the share of profits in US national income fell from the late 1960s. Arguing that the Keynesian demand-side models do not explain this 'profit squeeze' and the consequent damper on investment, Bhaduri and Marglin propose a composite model that includes the double-edged effect of the real wage on capital formation.

On the one hand wages are a cost. The higher the real wage rate, *ceteris paribus*, the lower the profit rate.[49] And the lower the profit rate, the lower the rate of investment, according to the classical view. So there is an inverse supply-side relationship between the investment spending and the real wage rate. On the other hand, from a post-Keynesian perspective, the propensity to consume from wage income is higher than it is from profit income, so higher wages mean greater aggregate demand and hence a higher rate of capacity utilization. Higher capacity utilization means higher profits as well as wages. So from the demand side, there is possibly a positive relationship between wages and investment.

More specifically, consider the following investment function:

$$g = I/K = i\,(r^{\,e})$$

where r^e is the expected rate of profit.[50] As in the post-Keynesian models, the expected rate of profit is a function of the actual profit rate. The latter can disaggregated into its components:

$$r = R/K = R/Y \,.\, Y/Y \,.\, Y/K = \Pi \,.\, z \,.\, a^{-1}$$

where Y is full capacity output, Π profit share in income, z the rate of capacity utilization, and 'a' the capital output ratio at full capacity. Taking 'a' as given, the investment function is

$$g = i(r^{\,e}\,\{\Pi, z\}\,)$$

The partial derivative of the expected profit rate with respect to each variable is positive. The real wage rate varies inversely with Π, which represents the supply side effect, and directly with z, which represents the Keynesian demand effect.

The model (of which this investment function is a part) depicts two possible basic scenarios. In the 'stagnationist' regime a lower profit share (higher wage share) leads to a higher rate of aggregate output, i.e. the demand effect dominates. In the 'exhilarationist' regime, a higher profit rate leads to a higher level of activity, i.e. the classical profit effect dominates. A more detailed taxonomy is possible, but all of these scenarios are necessarily hypothetical (Marglin and Bhaduri 1991: 145). It is the relative responsiveness of investment (and savings) to Π and z that determines which regime will come about. The model does not explain this relative responsiveness, which, as in the post-Keynesian models, depends on 'animal spirits'. This is arguably a more complete and explicit representation than the others described above, since it includes both the cost effect and the demand effect of the wage rate on investment spending. However, as the authors themselves emphasize, it is indeterminate to the point that anything can be made to happen by giving arbitrary values to the coefficients.

With respect to 'animal spirits', Bhaduri and Marglin seem to think that the device of subjective probabilities, used extensively in the neoclassical literature, is useful in emphasizing 'the state of mind of the investor as a crucial determinant of investment demand' (1991: 135). But in their own model, as in numerous neoclassical models that rely on this concept, the 'state of the mind of the investor' is not a subject of study; it is simply assumed. The neoclassical models assume economic agents act as if they base their decisions on a neoclassical general equilibrium model with contingent commodity markets. Such markets 'have the effect of eliminating the investor's state of mind from the investment-decision process' (ibid.).

This neoclassical assumption sidesteps the uncomfortable fact pointed out by Keynes, that investment decisions are about the distant future but we usually have no basis for predicting that future. By contrast, models with a Keynesian orientation, as we have seen, emphasize the arbitrariness of the expectations which underlie these decisions. But expectations that refer back to the theory itself are not unique to neoclassical models. Keynesian economic agents form expectations arbitrarily, since their assumed state of mind has to be in accordance with the Keynesian approach if the latter is a valid explanation. In other words, Keynesian models of investment are plausible if economic agents base their decisions on a Keynesian model. But in that case, they are forming their expectations arbitrarily.

In their interpretation of the experience of recent decades, Bhaduri and Marglin point out that any public policy aimed at influencing investment decisions can be counteracted and rendered ineffective by investor expectations (1991: 158). Suppose investors are using the Bhaduri-Marglin investment function with unknown coeficients in making decisions. Since the model is indeterminate, agents act on the assumption that policy results will be indeterminate. Their reaction is then arbitrary.

3.7   CONCLUSION

The premise that investors' state of mind is all-important but exogenous to economics has a logical conclusion that runs through different types of post-Keynesian growth models. Keynesian investors do whatever they feel like doing, and the models reflect this arbitrariness. Tobin (1975) pointed out that if agents perceive the economy in Keynesian terms, that is if they have Keynesian 'rational expectations', these expectations will lead to Keynesian outcomes. If chapter 12 of the *General Theory* and sundry remarks by post-Keynesians on expectations are taken seriously, these expectations can be anything and are not amenable to systematic investigation. This chapter shows how Keynesian explanations of investment and growth are undermined by this arbitrariness.

Of course, mainstream Keynesians (such as Tobin) did not follow this route. Instead, they ignored chapter 12 and allied Keynesian macroeconomics to neoclassical microeconomics. In the 1980s this synthesis became extremely lopsided, with what little there was of Keynes overwhelmed by neoclassical theory. We will now turn to the latter.

4 Neoclassical Models: Unbounded Rationality

4.1 OPTIMAL CAPITAL ACCUMULATION

Neoclassical models of investment define investment in two ways. Investment is demand for durable capital goods on the one hand, and on the other it is the supply of savings. The basic neoclassical view of the demand for a capital good is that, like the demand for everything else, it is a function of its relative price. Investment is the acquisition, at a given point of time, of capital goods which contribute services to production at different points of time. The passage of time means that the interest rate is part of the price, commonly called the 'user cost' of capital services.

The decision to acquire a capital asset and obtain a stream of productive services from it is analyzed as the solution to the problem of maximizing an intertemporal stream of consumption, which implies maximization of the present value of the firm (Jorgenson 1969: 214). There are variations on this story, but the basic logic is the same in different versions of the model. The objective function is the firm's present value, that is, the integral over time of discounted net receipts (Jorgenson 1969: 217–22). The constraint is the production function. The solution of the maximization problem yields the familiar marginal productivity condition

$$dQ/dK = c/p$$

where c is the user cost of capital services. This condition, which holds at each point in time, is identical to the marginal productivity condition of the static theory of the firm, except that the latter holds only at a single point in time. The similarity reflects the formal analogy between intertemporal and atemporal general equilibrium theory (Jorgenson 1989). The user cost of capital services is the price that the firm should charge itself and can be specified in terms of its components, namely the nominal interest rate, the expected rate of inflation, depreciation of capital goods, and taxes.[1]

The optimum level of capital services for each period is thus determined by the marginal productivity conditions and the production function. The 'desired' stock of capital for the period is the stock that will generate this level of capital services. Given the usual assumptions about the production function, the optimum level of capital services is an inverse function of user cost. The desired stock of capital for a given level of output is therefore an inverse function of user cost.

Haavelmo (1960) argued that deriving the desired capital stock from the profit maximization problem is insufficient to determine the demand for investment goods. There is the further issue of the adjustment of the actual capital stock to the desired level. The commonly accepted solution is to assume that investment is proportional to the difference between the existing stock and the desired stock of capital. This does not change the end result, which is that at a given level of income investment varies inversely with the user cost of capital, where the latter includes the interest rate. Investment varies directly with the price of the product. In an intertemporal model, the prices are forward prices.

For our purposes, one feature of this theory is particularly noteworthy. It depends on an exogenously specified technology. That is, the marginal productivity conditions in general and the condition for capital in particular, depend on a given, fully defined, production function. Investment is a function of the production function, but the latter is independent of investment, within the confines of the model. The production set has to be stable for the optimization problem to have a solution. Implicitly, the relationship between capital formation and its technological effects is assumed away. Insofar as capital formation is regarded as an allocation problem like any other allocation problem, investment decisions can be analyzed within the confines of the static theory of the firm.

This neoclassical model sidesteps the issue of the unknown future return on investment raised by Keynes. The marginal product of capital is well-defined, exogenously given, and known, because the production function is well-defined, exogenously given, and known. The issue of uncertainty and the possibility of endogenous changes in the production function are simply ignored. Hence this type of investment model can be characterized as an application of the static profit-maximizing hypothesis, with very little connection to growth and technical change.

Other neoclassical models explicitly account for uncertainty. In these, the firm maximizes its mean present value subject to a stochastically shifting industry demand (Lucas and Prescott 1971). An investment decision can be thought of as a contingency plan that shows the firm's reaction to a possible configuration of future prices. The investment decision requires forecasts of output prices as the demand for the products shifts randomly each period. The neoclassical models of investment under uncertainty simply assume that the firm knows the 'true' distribution of prices for all future periods.

Specifically, the conceptual basis of this treatment of investment under uncertainty can be described in two parts. One, agents know the probability distribution of relevant variables and use a neoclassical model of the economy in making decisions. Two, this model assumes that 'the stochastic component of demand has a regular, stationary structure' (Lucas and Prescott 1971: 664 n.9). Hence agents, like the model, assume that future shifts take place within a 'stationary structure'. While the first part raises issues about agents' ability to know, learn, and compute, the second part is an assumption not only about economic agents but about their environment. The environment is subject to random shifts, but the pattern of these shifts is given and stable; investment decisions do not affect this pattern. In effect, the model incorporates uncertainty about the future by assuming away uncertainty about future changes.

This is a logical implication of the neoclassical concept of uncertainty used in various other contexts as well as in investment models. The set of the possible states of the world is well defined and exogenously given. The uncertainty is only about which state of the world will come about. The exogeneity, as we will see later, is a crucial element. Future states of the world and their probabilities are defined independently of agents' decisions.

In effect, the models deal with uncertainty by assuming there is a function that cranks out future states. This function is exogenously given. It has an error term and the probability distribution of this error term is also given. Clearly this is an assumption about the world in general, not only about agents' knowledge or abilities. Optimization is possible under uncertainty in this framework, because future possibilities exist as blueprints, and the blueprint with the highest expected value can be chosen. This is what makes possible the analysis of investment as an optimization problem. The firm maximizes expected present value, given the distribution of possible future shifts.

4.2 GROWTH WITH EXOGENOUS TECHNICAL CHANGE

Neoclassical growth models say little about investment behaviour *per se*. These models do not contain a separate investment function, as A. Sen (1970) has pointed out. The one-sector Solow-Swan model, which is the basis for more complicated growth exercises, simply assumes that investment is equal to savings and takes the savings rate as given.[2] Later versions incorporate time preference as the determinant of saving behavior. This amounts to taking society's degree of patience in waiting for consumption as given, instead of the savings propensity. The greater a society's willingness to postpone consumption, the higher, *ceteris paribus*, its savings and investment rate. In a sense this is a tautological relationship: the more a society saves, the more 'patient' it must be. Questions such as what makes one society more patient than another or changes in time preference from one period to another are beyond the scope of growth models, though some authors offer *ad hoc* empirical explanations. Within the theoretical structure, time preference is data, like all preferences.

The basic neoclassical growth model is based on the conventional well-behaved production function. Labor-augmenting technical change at an exogenously given constant proportional rate, m, can be inserted into the production function:

$$Y = F(K, A(t)L)$$

where $A(t)$ is a function of time and changes at the rate m. Output per worker (y) and capital per worker (k) are measured in efficiency units:

$$y = Y/A(t)L \qquad k = K / A(t)L$$

The rate of growth of the capital labor ratio can be shown to be:

$$dk / k = sf(k) - (n + m)k$$

where (n) is standard notation for the rate of growth of the actual labor force, and (m) is the rate of labor augmenting technical change. The sum ($n + m$) measures the growth of the effective labor force, due to the increase in the number of workers and to labor-augmenting exogenous technical change. As shown in Figure 4.1, the capital labor ratio k^* is a stable growth equilibrium where:

$$sf(k) = (n + m)k.$$

In this steady state, the capital stock and output grow at rate ($n + m$). A notable and counter-intuitive result of this framework is that investment ($sf(k)$) has no effect on the long-run growth rate of the capital stock or output.

The characterization of technical change as purely labor-augmenting, that is, as Harrod neutral, is necessary for the existence of a stable equilibrium growth rate for capital stock and output. As Solow emphasizes: 'There must be a way of measuring employment in efficiency units so that the underlying technological relationship between output and employment for given capital stock is unchanged from year to year *when employment is measured in efficiency units*' (1970: 34. Italics in original).

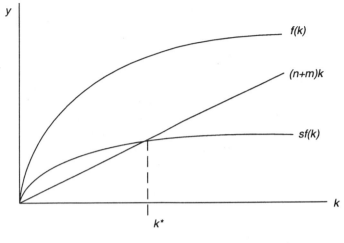

Figure 4.1

The productivity of labor, as measured in efficiency units, is '*dependent on the passage of time, but not on the stock of capital,* so that the input–output curve doesn't change at all in that system of measurement' (Solow 1970: 35).

The main requirement for tractability that Solow thus establishes is a stationary $f(k)$. There are other requirements. To ensure the existence of a steady state growth path, $(n + m)k$ has to pass through the origin. To ensure its uniqueness, $(n + m)k$ has to be linear. The austere determinateness of the Solow-Swan model is extremely fragile. A violation of any of these assumptions can destroy the existence, uniqueness, and/or stability of the steady-state growth path. The key premise that provides the desirable characteristics is that technical progress takes place at an exogenously given, constant and proportional rate.

Commenting on the idea of an exponential rate of growth of technical knowledge, J. Schmookler wrote: 'Few ideas have proved so intuitively attractive with so little foundation in either logic or evidence' (1966: 59).[3] Even if technical progress is assumed to be exogenous, a variety of possible growth scenarios can be constructed. For example, Figure 4.2 shows a scenario where:

$$n + m = 0 \quad \text{for} \quad y < y'$$

Below the threshold y', extreme poverty prevents productivity and population growth. Population explodes (i.e. n takes a high value) at some (y) above (y'). As a result there is no steady state growth path. Poverty traps that approximate this situation are not unknown in low-income countries. Other scenarios that allow (*n*) to take more than one value are just as plausible as the situation depicted in Figure 4.1.

The point is, the model provides no way to compare possible growth scenarios and no indication of what might cause one rather than another. It simply assumes one particular type of growth, but the assumed scenario is no more plausible than others. Possible complications were (and to a large extent still are) sequestered in the messy world of development economics and economic history. Why should a theory purporting to explain growth be irrelevant for development? The arbitrary assumptions made for the sake of tractability are an obvious explanation.

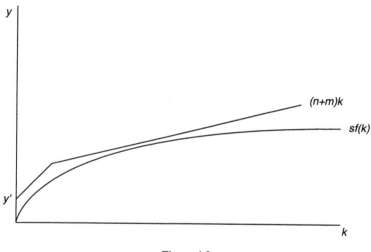

Figure 4.2

If (*m*) is not exogenous but is a function of (*k*), this basic neoclassical growth model loses its explanatory power. Movements along $f(k)$ cannot be distinguished from shifts of the function if (*m*) depends on (*k*). In effect, the production function cannot be defined.

The assumption of exogenous technical change, perhaps initially acceptable as a starting-point, appeared increasingly unsatisfactory. Attempts at improving growth theory took the form of treating technical change as an endogenous variable dependent on capital accumulation. However, the tractability requirement of stable functions remained, and later neoclassical growth exercises made other assumptions about technical change in order to meet this requirement, as we shall see.

A word on other antecedents to current growth models is in order. Vintage models also take the rate of growth of technical knowledge as exogenous, but show the embodiment of technology by assigning a date to each piece of physical capital. A machine embodies the level of technology at the time of its construction, and the capital stock is the sum of machines of different vintages. The main result derived from vintage models is that the long-run equilibrium rate of growth of output is independent of the rate of savings and investment, just as in the basic Solow-Swan model. Embodiment makes no difference to equilibrium growth because there is a constant age distribution of capital stock on the steady-state path. The rate of technical change is independent of the age distribution of the capital stock.[4]

The Kennedy-Weizacker invention possibility frontier shows the trade-off between capital-augmenting and labor-augmenting inventions.[5] The frontier, as to be expected, is concave to the origin like the good old production possibility frontier. Given factor prices, it is possible to determine an optimal choice of bias in technical change. Its pace, however, is not determined by the model. The frontier itself is as much manna from heaven as the exogenous rate of technical change assumed in the Solow-Swan model, and is not related to the rate of capital accumulation. The various versions of neoclassical growth theory are subject to the same objections put forth in this chapter against the basic logical structure, and are omitted from further discussion in order to avoid repetition.

4.3   NEW CLASSICAL GROWTH PARABLES: INTRODUCTION

In the 1980s growth theory rose from the ashes of its former incarnation, much like the phoenix. In a sense, the new wave of models are hybrids that graft the post-Keynesian Nicholas Kaldor's stylized facts and technical progress function onto the neoclassical framework. The theoretical development of earlier neoclassical growth models petered out in mathematical sterility during the 1970s. In the meantime, the empirical growth-accounting literature flourished, measuring the contributions to productivity growth of different factors of production in ever greater detail. The growth models and the growth 'accounts' had the same conceptual underpinning, but the models did not seem as relevant for actual growth experience.[6] No more. The current crop of new classical models claim historical relevance and have policy implications.[7]

Kaldor's approach to growth, as explained in the previous chapter, can be considered Keynesian on the grounds that it determines investment independently of saving behavior. The share of savings in national output is a function of the share of investment. Kaldor's technical progress function showed the relationship between capital accumulation and productivity growth, given the 'degree of inventiveness' of the economy. This relationship determined the equilibrium rate of investment, which in turn determined the savings propensity. The new classical models are in the neoclassical tradition, in the sense that investment spending is a function of savings behaviour rather than vice versa. The common idea behind the Kaldor model and the neoclassical growth models of Scott and Romer discussed in the next sections is that capital accumulation gives rise to technical change and technical change provides the incentive for capital accumulation.

This treatment of technical change distinguishes the first generation neoclassical models from the second generation. Technical change is endogenously determined by the rate of investment spending, more or less along the lines of the technical progress function. The exact nature of this determination varies from author to author, but there is a common approach to technical change, which I will refer to as the steady state approach.

Two examples of the recent growth literature are examined below. Each of these models illustrates an aspect of the steady state approach to technical change. The Scott (1989) model shows what this approach means for the modeling of investment spending. In order to determine a steady-state growth path, restrictions have to be placed on how technical change affects investment opportunities. The treatment of technical change by Romer (1990) raises issues about what we mean by new knowledge, its production and its use. An examination of these models points to problems that stem from the same source, and lead to the same general conclusion. Steady-state modeling requires the imposition of arbitrary restrictions on endogenous technical change, just as it required Harrod-neutral exogenous technical change in the Solow-Swan model. The result is that the neoclassical endogenous technical change models are unsatisfactory for the same reason that Kaldor's technical progress function was unsatisfactory. In a later section, I argue that the restrictions imposed by the steady-state approach are not justified by the stylized facts of growth.

4.4   INVESTMENT AS CHANGE

Understanding growth requires understanding the two-way relationship between investment and technical change. Investment promotes innovation and diffusion, while innovation opens up new investment opportunities.[8] Growth accounting exercises do not allow for interaction between factors of production and technical change. In order to attribute parts of the growth rate to separate factors and the residual to technical change, such exercises implicitly assume that capital, labor and technical change make separate and additive contributions to growth. A large part of the agenda for recent growth exercises is to include the interactive relationship.

It is M. Scott's innovation to merge capital formation and technical change, getting rid of the distinction between them altogether. In the Scott model material investment is defined as expenditure 'undertaken to change and hopefully improve economic arrangements in excess of required maintenance' (Scott 1989: 15). R&D expenditures are included in this definition.[9] The only other type of investment is human investment. The growth of output is a function of material investment, human investment and the growth of the labor force. Technical change does not appear as a separate variable.

Scott's basic model does not have a conventional production function, that is, a relationship between output and inputs. Instead it consists of relationships between growth rates: the growth of labor in natural and quality-adjusted units; the growth of output; and the rate of investment. The discussion here will focus on one part of the model, namely the treatment of investment. Other aspects, that are not directly related to the critique developed here, are ignored. The interested reader will have to consult Scott (1989) for the full story.

Each investment project is characterized by change of output per unit investment (q) and change in labor input per unit investment (l). Projects that yield a higher increase in output (higher q) for given or lower labor input are more profitable than projects with lower q. Thus the points to the north-west in Figure 4.3 show projects that are relatively more profitable than those to the south-east. There may be any number (h_i) of investment projects with the same q_i, l_i. If the h_i's are thought of as a third dimension rising up from Figure 4.3, the set of investment opportunities can be visualized as a 'cake' sitting on the 'plate' of q-l space. The 'cake' is asymmetrical. Scott argues that the projects thin out to the north-west, since at a given time there is a limited number of investments that can yield a relatively high rate of return, whereas there are many low profitability projects, so the h_i's are higher toward the south-east.

The share of material investment in output is determined by the marginal real rate of return on investment and the discount rate at which marginal

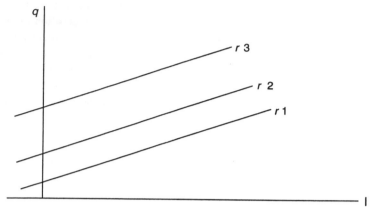

Figure 4.3

consumption is discounted. The real rate of return on investment is

$$r = P(q - \lambda l)$$

where P is the price level and λ the wage share. The latter is determined in the labor market, the former is taken as numeraire. The locus of q_i and l_i that give the same rate of return is a Equal Profit Contour (EPC). The EPCs denote higher rates of return the further one moves to the north-west. That is,

$$r3 > r2 > r1$$

in Figure 4.3.

The 'cake' of investment opportunities may be a novel metaphor, but the behavioral assumptions of this model are not different from those of other neoclassical investment and growth models. Investors maximize the present value of returns. The investment projects that have a rate of return higher than or equal to the social discount rate are undertaken. In terms of Scott's metaphor, the EPC at the social discount rate cuts a piece of cake to the north-west of itself. This subset of investment projects determines the share of investment in output.

Dynamic equilibrium is a steady-state growth path along which the growth rates of various variables and the share of investment in output remain constant. The existence of such a path requires that the shape of the investment opportunities 'cake' remain constant. Scott assumes that the set of investment opportunities is continually recreated so that the aggregate investment undertaken at the same rate of return has the same average q and l. In other words, for each period the same number of investment projects (h_i) with the same characteristics q_i and l_i are available. He argues that this is a 'reasonable working hypothesis' on two grounds (1989: 159):

1. The stylized facts of growth suggest that historically there has been no exhaustion of investment opportunities. I will discuss the possible interpretations of the stylized facts in a later section.
2. Investment leads to learning and thus recreates investment opportunities.

The second point is actually tangential to Scott's assumption. Given that the definition of investment used in the model includes technical change, there is no issue that investment creates investment opportunities. The issue is whether the relationship between q and l remains constant as investment and technical change proceed. Another way of putting the assumption is that the implicit function that specifies the relationship between labor input changes (l) and output changes (q) is exogenously given and in particular is independent of technical change. It is hard to think of a real-world reason why the relationship between l and q should be independent of technical change. This assumption is no more justifiable than the assumption of earlier growth models that technical change is independent of investment. Both assumptions are made for theoretical convenience, that is, to ensure the existence of a steady-state growth path.

Scott's model has the virtue of showing clearly what is involved in determining a steady-state path in the presence of endogenous technical change. He attempts to qualify the assumption of a constant set of investment opportunities by noting that it is a matter for empirical investigation, not 'a law of nature' (1989: 162). But there is a theory-generated dilemma here, and it is not confined to the Scott model. The same dilemma shows up in different guises in all steady-state models of growth. For an equilibrium path to exist, the functions that define equilibrium have to be stable. The functional forms and the parameters have to be constant along the path. A change in the functions causes a shift to another path. Within the steady-state framework, even to study the effects of such shifts an equilibrium growth rate has to be determined. In itself, this sounds familiar and innocuous. In the context of growth, however, it has a not so innocuous implication. The functions, however defined, have to be independent of technical change. This means that even in models where technical change is formally endogenous, it has to take place in an exogenously specified way, just as Kaldor's production function for technical change is exogenous. We saw that Solow assumed Harrod-neutral technical change for the sake of theoretical tractability. Scott's specification of the investment opportunities set, if it is to have any theoretical usefulness, requires another neutrality assumption, namely that technical change be 'neutral' with respect to investment opportunities.

There is a second issue related to the constancy of the investment opportunities set. Scott discusses investment projects as if there were full information on the q_i and l_i for each project. He argues that only the current values of these magnitudes need to be considered in the model. But of course the decision-making agents have to consider the changes in output and labor input over the lifetime of the investment. The assumption that the set of potential investments does not change takes care of the informational issue.[10] Since the same set of opportunities exists for a long time, agents learn the investment map. This means that the supposedly dynamic model is structurally static. Agents learn the 'true' investment opportunities and rates of return because the structure of the economy, and hence the set of opportunities, is stationary.

A necessary complementary assumption is that agents receive correct feedbacks, so that their expectations converge to the 'true' set of opportunities. These interlinked assumptions of constant investment opportunities and 'correct' learning guarantee theory-consistent expectations. Theory-consistent expectations are necessary both for the existence of the steady-state path and for its stability. Without these assumptions, the model is indeterminate.

4.5   KNOWLEDGE AS EXTERNALITY

The series of models developed by Romer around the concepts of increasing returns and monopolistic competition represent the most comprehensive treatment of endogenous technical change within the neoclassical framework.[11]

Romer defines technical knowledge as a 'design' that can be used over and over again with no depreciation. The cost of developing a design is similar to incurring a fixed cost (1990: S72). Each design is used to produce a capital good, and the owner of the design fully appropriates the return from this use. But designs also have spillover effects by contributing to the common pool of technical knowledge that researchers use in producing new designs. The owner has no way of controlling the design's contribution to general knowledge, and cannot appropriate the returns due to this contribution. Thus technology has a dual character. As design for producer good, it is a income-yielding asset produced by profit-maximizing agents; as knowledge it is an externality. This duality makes it possible to model technical change as the outcome of conventional capital accumulation, but not subject to the diminishing returns that capital deepening would otherwise bring, given the usual neoclassical assumptions about production. Instead, technology is subject to increasing returns, as Romer illustrates with the following thought experiment. Given a set of designs, doubling all other inputs doubles output. But this means that doubling the designs as well as all other inputs more than doubles output. If the increasing returns are postulated to be external to firms, the assumption of perfect competition can be retained. More realistically, design producing firms can be characterized as subject to increasing returns and monopolistic competition (Romer 1990).

In the Romer 1990 model there are four inputs: physical capital (x), human capital (H), physical labor (L), and 'an index of the level of technology' which is referred to as the stock of technical knowledge (A). A 'unit of knowledge' corresponds to a 'design', and the stock of knowledge is therefore the total number of designs. One of the questions raised by this treatment is the measurement of the stock of knowledge, (A), to which we will return. I will first describe salient elements of the model, then evaluate the assumptions about investment and technical change.

The research sector produces new knowledge, i.e. designs, using the public stock of knowledge and human capital. The assumption, noted above, is that anybody engaged in research has free access to the entire stock of knowledge (A). The production function for designs, based on this assumption, is:

$$\mathrm{d}\,A\,/\,\mathrm{d}\,t = \delta\,H_A\,A \tag{4.1}$$

where H_A is the human capital employed in research. Physical capital is disaggregated into an infinite number of distinct types of producer durables, each corresponding to a design. The final goods sector uses producer goods, human capital, and labor. Output in this sector is an additively separable function of producer durables (x_i):

$$Y\,(H_Y, L, x) = H_Y{}^{\alpha}\,L^{\beta}\sum_{i=0}^{\infty}x_i{}^{1-\alpha-\beta} \tag{4.2}$$

At a given time, some producer durables have not been invented, i.e. some designs are yet to be developed. Hence there is some value of A such that

$$x_i = 0 \quad \text{for all } i > A$$

Final output Y can be either consumed or saved as new capital. The intermediate sector converts n units of final output used as capital (K) into one unit of producer durable i, on the basis of the design for i, for $i=1...A$. In this intermediate sector firms use each design to produce a distinctive producer good. The relationship between aggregate capital and the durable goods is

$$K = n. \; \Sigma_{i=0}{}^{\infty} \, x_i \qquad\qquad (4.3)$$

The production functions for the three sectors and the Ramsey utility function determine the steady state rate of growth (g) for consumption, output, capital stock and knowledge. The solution for the optimization problem is:

$$g = (\delta \, H - \Lambda \, p) \, / \, (\sigma. \, \Lambda + 1) \qquad\qquad (4.4)$$

where p is the social discount rate, σ the intertemporal rate of substitution, and Λ a constant that depends on the production parameters α and β.

The main result of this analysis is straightforward: the larger the human capital endowment and the lower the discount rate, the faster is equilibrium growth. The message with respect to preference parameters p and σ is a familiar one. The more patient a society, i.e. the lower the discount rate p, the higher the rate of investment in research, and therefore higher the growth rate. Similarly, a higher intertemporal rate of substitution (lower σ) means a higher steady state growth rate.

4.6   STEADY STATES IN AN UNSTEADY WORLD

Again, the key to this growth model is the specification of the production functions. Once stable functions are specified, determining the steady-state path that maximizes net final output is a straightforward exercise. As Romer writes: 'because (A) changes as new producer durables are invented, it is important to be able to describe final output as *a stationary function* of all conceivable input lists' (Romer 1990: S80; emphasis added). As we saw, this applies to all steady-state growth models: Stationary functions are necessary to determine the equilibrium rate of the growth. Hence the functions have to be exogenous, that is, have to independent of growth and technical change. This is so whether the function is a knowledge production function *à la* Romer, an investment opportunities set *à la* Scott, a conventional production function *à la* Solow, or technical progress function *à la* Kaldor. In the context of the Romer (1990) model described in the previous section, the theoretically required stationariness means that technical change has no effect on:

1.   The functional forms (i.e. equations 4.1, 4.2, and 4.3.)
2.   The production coefficients (in particular δ, α and β)
3.   The units in which the stock of knowledge (A) is measured.

The three conditions may seem so obvious and in keeping with conventional neoclassical reasoning as not to merit attention. All that is required is that the functional forms, parameters and units of measurement be exogenous. However, in the present context these requirements are noteworthy, for they impose a peculiar and arbitrary structure on technical change. I will discuss each of the three requirements in turn.

Consider equation (4.2). As the number of designs in existence increase from 0 to ∞ along the growth path, the additively separable function that represents the production of final goods is unchanged, that is, the relationship between capital goods continues to be additively separable. New technologies that change this relationship, by introducing new complementarities and substitution possibilities between capital goods, are ruled out. For example, as new computer designs are introduced, the relationship between computers and other inputs in the production of final goods remains unchanged. The issue here is, of course, not the specific form of equation (4.2) but the constancy of whatever form is assumed. This constancy rules out certain types of innovation.

The production of designs is similarly impervious to the level of development of technology. The relationship between human capital and knowledge is the same whether the knowledge is about slide rules or about computers. The introduction of computers does not bring new substitution possibilities or complementarities in research that can change equation (4.1) and the production coefficient δ. Technical change has to be neutral to functional forms and parameters, for the same reason that it had to be exogenous and purely labor-augmenting in the Solow-Swan model.

What real-life innovation could take place in such a neutral fashion? The answer is obvious: incremental changes in technology that usually take place without bringing new substitution possibilities and without requiring new complementarities among inputs.[12] The development of a slightly different computer model is unlikely to change the production parameters or the shape of the production function for computers or other products. The shift from slide rule to computer does. What the stationariness in effect means is that discontinuities in technology are beyond the explanatory scope of the theory, where 'discontinuity' is defined as any change that violates the stationariness of functions, parameters, and the unit of measurement of technical knowledge. Such innovations can take place exogenously and cause a shift to a new steady-state path. But investment in the production of designs cannot result in technological discontinuities. If it does, the functions become unstable.

Kaldor's technical progress function had a similar requirement that technical change take place without causing changes in the function itself. If movements along the function cause changes in the function, the function cannot be specified, and no equilibrium can be determined. In the recent crop of growth models, too, innovations that cause changes in functional forms or parameters have to be exogenous to ensure the existence of the steady-state path. The endogeneity of technical change in steady state models is more apparent than real. Except for a particular type of incremental innovation that takes place according to the given functions, technical change still has to be exogenous for the sake of theoretical tractability. In the new growth models discontinuous technical change falls from heaven or the ivory tower, just as Harrod-neutral technical change did in the Solow-Swan model.

The same conclusion follows if we consider the third requirement. The stock of knowledge (A) is measured in number of 'designs'. What the unit is called is a matter of semantics: 'design' is as good as 'blueprint' or 'patent'. No matter what word is used, there is a conceptual issue. The unit has to remain constant as the number of designs in existence increase from zero to infinity. Otherwise, (A) will change not only because knowledge is growing but because the unit of account is changing. That is, unless the unit is constant, there will be nominal changes in the stock of knowledge in addition to real changes. The only way to separate out the real changes in knowledge from nominal changes in the unit of account is to use a third variable as an index of changes in the unit. There is, however, no such independent index to measure changes in a unit of technical knowledge. If what is meant by a unit of knowledge changes, it will not be possible to use (A) as an argument of the production function, since doubling (A) may not mean there is twice as much knowledge. It is necessary for the unit to remain constant, if the production function of designs (equation 4.1) is to be logically coherent.

Small incremental changes in existing technology may not cause complications of this sort. The introduction of a new computer model is unlikely to change what is meant by a 'design'. The change from slide rule to computer, however, brings changes in the specification of a design. Designs become more complicated and include information that previous designs did not contain. Since there is more diversity among computers than among slide rules, the concept of design itself changes.

Romer wisely assumes that designs do not become obsolete. Had he not taken refuge in this assumption, the measurement problem would have shown up in full force. A Schumpeterian discontinuity in technology could cause the unit of account to change in a perverse way. If the discontinuity comes in the form of a single new design that renders obsolete a number of old designs, (A) will shrink even as technical knowledge expands. The static counterpart of this phenomenon for physical capital, called 'reverse capital deepening', was a familiar issue in the 1960s capital controversies.[13] In the present context perverse changes in the stock of knowledge are perhaps more accurately described as 'false reverse learning'. A real-life example that comes to mind is the invention of the polio vaccine, which replaced a cumbersome set of treatments for polio victims. These pre-vaccine treatments included the iron lung and special physical therapy, and would be represented by a relatively larger number of designs than the simple vaccine. The invention of the vaccine, a leap in technology, would then have caused a decrease in (A).[14]

The conclusion is the same as for the requirement for functional and parametric stability. The steady state approach in general and its neoclassical variants in particular can endogenize only a certain type of incremental improvement in technology. What these models require is that technical change take place within an unchanging structure. Innovations that violate this requirement have to be exogenous and not very frequent if the models are to be of much use in explaining real life growth. As is to be expected, an unsteady world wreaks havoc on the determinateness of steady state growth models.

4.7 THEORY-CONSISTENT EXPECTATIONS

The three conditions discussed in the previous section are necessary for the stability of the steady-state growth path as well as for its existence. Theoretically correct investment decisions require that agents know the functional forms and parameters. The investment decision is not distinguished from the savings decision in neoclassical growth models. Hence investment is the decision to forego consumption of one unit of final good now in order to receive $(1 + r)$ units next period. The interest rate r is a function of the preference parameters (the social discount rate and the intertemporal rate of substitution) and the production parameters α, β, and δ. Divergences from the steady state growth rate g will be corrected if agents make investment decsions in accordance with the production parameters. This is plausible only if the functions are stable enough for agents to learn them. Lucas argues that rational expectations (RE) depend on acquisition of relevant knowledge by a sufficient number of economic agents so that others are also forced to behave in accordance with the correct functions or lose in competition (Lucas 1987). For this acquisition of knowledge to be possible, the functions have to be constant during the period under consideration.

In cycle models where RE were first applied, there may be no particular reason for the underlying relations to change. The application of the same concept to growth involves imposing the same stability requirement on technical change. Learning is possible if agents get reliable feedbacks about the results of their past behavior (Tversky and Kahnemann 1990), and this reliability in turn depends on the environment being unchanging so that agents can isolate the results of their own decisions. Even if a steady-state growth path exists, if one or more of the three conditions discussed above are violated, theory-consistent expectations cannot be taken for granted, and the stability of the path becomes questionable.

4.8 STYLIZED FACTS REVISITED

Growth theory, like all theory, is necessarily abstract. Kaldor argued that the choice of what is to be abstracted from should be based on broad empirical tendencies relevant for the problem, and suggested a set of 'stylized' facts that growth theory should explain.[15] Current theorists accept these, with some revisions. Two are relevant for the discussion in this section: a steady trend-rate of growth of labor productivity and a constant capital–output ratio. In accordance with this empirical generalization, models determine equilibrium growth paths, on which the growth rate, productivity growth, and the capital output ratio are constant. Obviously, this generalization is highly convenient from a theoretical point of view, as it justifies the application of equilibrium reasoning and tools to growth.

In the previous sections I have questioned the appropriateness of the steady state framework as applied to the relationship between investment and technical change. The stylized facts provide the starting point and the empirical justification for steady-state growth theory. To question the conceptual framework implies rethinking the stylized facts.

Two of the items on Kaldor's original list, namely the continuous growth of capital per worker and the constant rate of return on capital, follow from the others. These two can be left out with no loss of information (Solow 1970; Romer 1989, section 2.1). Another fact, the constancy of capital and labor shares in national income, appears to be questionable, as most time series suggest that capital's share has fallen over the past century.[16] Romer confirms the remaining three 'facts':

1. Output per worker grows at a steady rate with no tendency to fall or rise.
2. The capital output ratio is steady.
3. There are wide differences between countries in rates of productivity growth.

Even if this list is taken to apply only to high income industrial economies, 'fact' number one is suspect. After all, there is a wide-spread impression that we are living in the midst of a long-run productivity growth slow-down. Romer denies that there is such a thing going on and claims that only a 'few most recent observations on a relatively noisy time series' give this impression.

Another interpretation that supports the first stylized fact is that the fall in the rate of productivity growth in all industrial economies since the early 1970s is merely the end of an extraordinary period of growth, a return to 'normal growth rates' (Baumol, Blackman and Wolff 1989: 65). It was the 1950s–60s high growth rates that were a historical aberration, probably representing a 'catch-up in the utilization of accumulated technological ideas – inventions whose utilization was held up by the Depression and war' (Baumol, Blackman and Wolff 1989: 70). These authors find that the trend rate of American productivity growth for 1880–1985 is an almost flat line (Figure 4.4).[17] The period 1950–85, in their view, is dominated by a 'long period cycle', with two periods of rising and one period of falling productivity growth (1989: 77).[18]

Figure 4.4 can be considered from two perspectives. One, the flat regression trend can be taken as evidence of steady long-run productivity growth, in keeping with the first stylized fact. The second possibility is to view the ups and downs as evidence of the unsteadiness of productivity growth, and explain it as a sequence of subperiods. This is the way a number of researchers, including Maddison (1982, 1991) and Scott (1989) interpret the historical experience: as a series of phases. The models described above can be thought of as explaining growth during a given

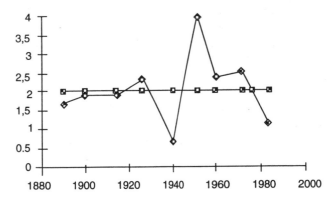

Figure 4.4   United States GDP per work-hour, growth states and trend line.
Source: Baumol, Blackman and Wolff 1989: 69.

phase, during which growth approximates the steady state. Shifts from one path to another are outside the theory's explanatory power. Scott (1989), for example, provides ad hoc explanations for such shifts.

Maddison (1991), adding more recent observations to the same time series, concludes that a slow-down has occurred since 1973. Maddison distinguishes three phases in the twentieth century. The period 1914–40 was one of extreme interruptions in growth. It was succeeded by the post-war secular boom, which ended in the early 1970s. According to Maddison, each phase is characterized by a different policy approach and institutional environment.

In the longer time horizon, say roughly during the last three centuries, a central feature of capitalist growth is the shift of productivity growth leadership from country to country. The 'lead' country in this context is the one operating closest to the technological frontier. This lead passed from the Netherlands to the UK in the nineteenth century, and from the latter to the US in the twentieth (Maddison 1991: graph 2-1). The reasons behind this change of the guard appear to be specific for each case.[19] Whereas the Netherlands fell into a prolonged stagnation due to the loss of its mono-poly position in world markets, 'The emergence of the US as the technical leader was due mainly to its large investment effort. The rate of US domestic investment was nearly twice the UK level for the sixty year period 1890–1950' (Maddison 1991: 40). This was not due to a relatively low savings rate in the UK; on the contrary, UK foreign investment was as large as domestic investment and British investment in the US contributed to the latter's growth. A similar dynamic may now be operating between Japan, where the ratio of gross fixed non-residential investment to GNP was 23.9 per cent in 1974–87, and the US, where the same ratio for this period was 13.6 per cent (Maddison 1991: 41, Table 2.3).

The issue is twofold. One part is the empirical issue of what is happen-ing. Is the apparent falling off of productivity growth a statistical illusion created by noise in the time series, as Romer asserts? Is it a return to the secular trend, as Baumol, Blackman and Wolf argue? Or is it more use-fully viewed as the latest turn of a generally unsteady secular growth rate? As industrial economies catch up with the productivity leader – the US – will growth rates tend to equalize? Such questions are probably not answer-able in the near future, but in so far as growth theory has pretentions of explaining real world growth, it has at least to ask them.

Assuming that there is indeed a secular change in productivity growth, the second part of the issue is whether the shift is systematic and endogenous. If the shift is due to random shocks and purely exogenous forces, the steady-state approach is a plausible way to study growth, at least as part of a more comprehensive approach which includes separate analyses of the shifts from one path to another. But if the shifts are not exogenous, this approach misses the central feature of growth. If the discontinuities are related to investment, understanding growth requires explaining this relationship. As we have seen, steady-state models have to assume away such endogeneity due to the tractability needs. Endogenous unsteadiness would cause the production function of technical knowledge (or the set of investment opportunities) to shift with capital accumulation. Endogenous shifts mean that movements along the function cannot be distinguished from shifts of the function, and that is another way of saying the function cannot be identified. An equilibrium growth path does not exist if the production sets shift due to capital accumulation, and the models are indeterminate. Hence steady-state models exclude such effects of investment.

Some historians paint a picture of growth that differs markedly from the steady-state scenario with exogenous shocks. Consider the following explanation of nineteenth-century American growth. According to Abramovitz and David (1973), US growth has taken place as 'a sequence of technologically induced traverses, disequilibrium transitions between successive growth paths' (429). Nineteenth-century American growth was due primarily to the increase of conventional inputs, physical capital and labor. The growth accounting 'residual' came into being in the twentieth century, as a result of previous growth. Technical change was biased, and the bias changed over time. It is this that explains secular changes in the economy. Nineteenth-century innovations were labor saving, which created demand for physical capital and led to a high return on investment. In the twentieth century technical change became capital enchancing, resulting in more demand for human capital and R&D. Hence investment in these unconventional types of capital increased while the rate of investment in physical capital declined.

In a related study, David (1977) identifies a 'Grand Traverse' from 1835 to 1890, during which the rate of investment accelerated, shunting the economy onto a different growth path.[20] David argues that much of the impetus came from the demand for investment rather than the supply of savings. This shift was not only in the growth rates, but also in the nature of growth. The traverse resulted in an economy which generates the momentum that is measured as the residual in growth accounting. David's study is based on comparative dynamics. The periods before and after the traverse, i.e., 1805–35 and 1890–1905, appear to be quasi-steady growth paths.

David's explanation of the traverse is shown in Figure 4.5. He argues that at the beginning of the nineteenth century the long-run supply of savings available in the United States for capital formation was extremely elastic in the relevant range, but potentially could become inelastic at a much higher rate of capital formation. On this supposition, the saving function has a horizontal segment followed by a vertical segment.[21] He also argues that the investment function was relatively inelastic (David 1977: 205–7). The capital-deepening bias in nineteenth-century innovations increased the demand for capital, shifting out the investment function (I/Y). This in itself would have led to a higher rate of return. David hypothesizes that simultaneously with the shift in investment there was a shift in the savings function. Technical change caused the relative price of investment goods to go down, increasing the investment that could be made for each unit of foregone consumption. Also the development of financial intermediaries increased the funds available for investment, contributing to the observed fall in the rate of return. David concludes:

> In every historical epoch of significant duration ... there has been a specific bias in the progress of invention.... The macroeconomic parables to be told about the way long-run development proceeded during these epochs should therefore be stories of non-steady growth for which 'balanced' expansion could only be an ephemeral phase soon to be disrupted by the progress of Invention [sic]... (222)

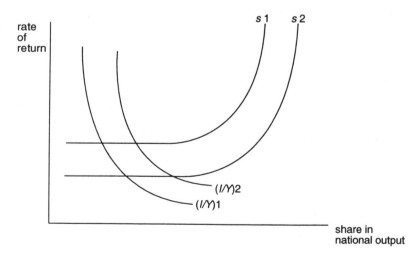

Figure 4.5

The concept of a steady-state path is, of course, useful in distinguishing such periods in this historical study. But these are insignificant episodes compared to the 55-year-long traverse. It is the latter that explains the emergence of the residual and the passing of productivity leadership from the UK to the US. The characteristics of the later period, i.e. 1890–1905, are determined by processes that took place during the traverse. The shifts of the functions are the main part of David's nineteenth-century parable.[22] To the extent that similar traverses are occurring in the twentieth century, models that center around steady-state growth simply miss the story.

What is perhaps more important is the less obvious point here. It is non-neutral technical change that disrupts steady growth in the early part of the nineteenth century. David notes that biased inventions were due to 'the opportunities of learning by doing which had been shaped by the past history of relative factor prices and the legacy of irreversible capital accumulation decisions' (1977: 214). The relationship between accumulation and technical change is endogenous, and the biases arising from past investments are also endogenous. Steady-state growth models express these relationships in terms of a production function for technical change. But that function cannot be stable if accumulation changes the relationship between inputs and outputs. If that is the case, movements along the function are causing shifts of the function. This is what makes for growth and development, and this is what equilibrium models assume away in order to investigate the properties of equilibrium growth.

To summarize, the historical record can be interpreted as a series of traverses connected by what looks like relatively steady growth periods. Non-neutral technical change occurs during phases of approximately steady growth, and leads to the next traverse. Models that depict steady growth do not advance our understanding either of the steady growth periods or the traverses, since the endogenous shifts that originate in the former and cause the latter are ignored or assumed to be exogenous. Otherwise, the tractability requirements of the models are compromised. In the light of the historical growth experience, equilibrium growth theory looks like *Hamlet* without the Prince.

4.9 CONCLUSION

This chapter started with a discussion of the stationary theory of investment most commonly found in intermediate macro and micro textbooks. The dynamic consequences of investment decisions are taken as exogenously given, embodied in future returns which are known when the decision is made. This is a schizophrenic treatment of investment. Investment is on the one hand a determinant of future productive capacity and an agent of change. On the other hand, the information on which it is based is simply assumed given, as if the unknown future had little to do with the decision to invest. Investment changes the future, while the explanation given stays firmly in the present and in effect assumes a stationary world.

We continued with the first generation of neoclassical growth models, where growth converged to an exogenously given natural rate. Finally, we considered the new generation growth models, where the relationship between technical change and investment is endogenous. However, the formal endogeneity obscures the substantive exogeneity that has to be assumed in order to establish the existence of the steady-state growth rate. Changes in the functions have to be exogenous for theoretical tractability. Steadiness is required for the existence of the equilibrium rate of growth as well as for its stability. Unless the functions are stable, it is not possible to determine a steady-state growth path. And shifts in the functions would not allow agents to learn the information required to make investment decisions consistent with the steady-state growth path. Investment decisions have to be based on correct information about the effects of the investments and these latter have to be incorporated into all market equilibria. The relationship between investment and technical change has to take place according to a specified function, which itself is subject only to exogenous changes.

Growth theorists' common appeal to stylized facts as the starting point of the models is not justified. Historical experience in itself, if it has not been censored and tailored to achieve (growth) theoretical correctness, does not justify the steady-state approach.

If the rate of investment is determined as an equilibrium, then disruptions of this equilibrium have to be exogenous. But technical change is a major force behind such disruptions, and is itself a result of investment. The solution to this theoretical dilemma has been to assume that innovation takes place in a neutral way, without causing unsteadiness. In effect, this means that any significant change in technology remains exogenous.

This approach to growth is rooted in the assumption of all-encompassing, unbounded rationality. Investment decisions are optimization problems and stable functions are required in solving an optimization problem. Without well-defined, steady functions, the optimum rate of capital accumulation and the equilibrium conditions cannot be determined. Optimization implies unbounded rationality, and imposes the tractability requirements discussed in this chapter.

Herbert Simon observes that the only gain from replacing exogenous technical change with a production function for innovation is 'that we can now rest comfortably in the knowledge that everything is proceeding rationally' (Simon 1984: 41–2). The exogeneity has merely been relocated from the rate of technical change to the parameters of the function. To build an interesting and useful theory of economic growth 'we have to go behind the principle of rationality' and specify the behavioral mechanisms that make agents invest in new technologies. To account for agents' beliefs about the outcomes of highly uncertain events, past experience has to be taken into account. The questions to be addressed include: What makes people pay attention to potential investment opportunities? What are the information and communication flows that underlie this attention? (Simon 1984: 53–4).

It may be objected that any other approach is impossible; and that the critique developed in this and previous chapters is nihilistic for theory. After all, if the future is unknown and relationships can change, all models will be indeterminate. The answer is that the type of determinateness steady-state analysis requires is not possible under the conditions that characterize real world growth. In other words, the concept of equilibrium is not particularly helpful in the study of investment and technical change. A possible alternative to the neoclassical and Keynesian models on this subject is the institutionalist approach, which is not organized around the concept of equilibrium. It therefore does not require that technical change be mathematically 'tractable', that is, amenable to standard optimization procedures that determine equilibrium conditions. The institutionalist approach, in its more recent incarnation, includes Schumpeterian, behaviorist and evolutionary elements. We will now consider this alternative.

5 Neo-institutionalism: Bounded Rationality

5.1 INTRODUCTION

The various models discussed in the preceding chapter rest on a certain definition of rationality, which can be characterized as 'unbounded' or 'hyperrationality'. In these models investment decisions are made according to calculations that span all possible states of the world for all relevant time periods. Rationality is thus all-encompassing, in the sense that there can be no endogenous surprises, though there can be exogenous shocks.[1] Barring events outside the explanatory power of the model, the menu of possibilities is given. In the growth and investment models presented in the previous chapter, unbounded rationality means that the technology and preference sets change only in predictable and pre-ordained ways. Therefore possible courses of action, that is, sequences of investments, and possible future states that follow from these investments, are defined and known. As was the case for David Ricardo, in modern neoclassical models investment opportunities are obvious, and it follows as a matter of course that the optimal path will be chosen. By contrast, the approach described in this chapter recognizes the limits to calculation. Instead of taking the choice set as given, it asks how the choice set is defined, what possible courses of action an agent will consider, and how agents' choices reshape the choice set.

I refer to this approach as neo-institutional economics with some misgivings. To be candid, there is no consensus on the boundaries and programmatic coherence of 'new institutional economics'.[2] The justification for this chapter is the existence of a substantial and promising body of research about (or relevant for) technical change that belongs neither to the neoclassical nor the Keynesian research program. Parts of this literature are variously referred to as neo-Schumpeterian, evolutionary, or behaviorist; part of it can best be described as the new economics of technical change, and an overlapping part falls under the rubric of business history.[3] Various writings focus on different questions and emphasize different explanations, but do have significant common features.

I use the term neo-institutionalist to describe a diverse group of researchers because this is a general and inclusive term that subsumes the other more narrowly defined labels. In this context 'evolutionary' means a method that seeks to explain the process rather than only the outcome. It does not imply the use of specific biological metaphors. Behaviorism is similarly defined in a general sense, as inquiry into the actual behavior of agents, as opposed to the use of *a priori* assumptions about behavior. Schumpeterian economics attributes a central role to technical change and points to conflicts between static and dynamic efficiency. By these definitions, new institutional economics has evolutionary, behaviorist, and Schumpeterian components.

The difficulty in delineating the boundaries of new institutional economics is partly due to questions about its relationship to the 'old' institutional economics, associated with the names of Thorstein Veblen, John Commons, Clarence Ayres, and currently represented by the *Journal of Economic Issues*. There is no basic conceptual incompatibility between the propositions described here and traditional institutionalist thinking.[4] There are differences between the 'old' and 'new' institutionalist economics, and there is a sharp divergence in policy implications. In particular, 'old' institutionalist economics tends to stress the negative aspects of corporate power without considering the productive potential of the institution.[5] The conceptual basis described in the next two sections is common to both old and new institutionalist work, but it is implicit in the former, while clearly elucidated and further developed in the latter.

Another part of the difficulty of defining an institutionalist research program is due to the recent proliferation of neoclassical explanations of institutions. Optimization-based treatments of institutions are an extension of the neoclassical research program, not an alternative approach, and hence should not be considered part of new institutional economics.[6] Some of the property-rights literature meets this description. Arguably some writers are neoclassical/institutionalist hybrids, such as Williamson (1985) and perhaps North (1990a, b). The latter does go beyond the neoclassical framework (and his own earlier writings) in recognizing long-term failure of market institutions as a possibility. A comprehensive methodological analysis as to what constitutes a distinct institutionalist research program is beyond this book. I take the pragmatic approach of drawing on a blend of explanations, including those based on transaction costs, rules of thumb behavior, evolutionary selection mechanisms, and the various patterns identified by historians of technical change and the firm. These are unified by the concept of bounded rationality. In the next two sections I will try to clarify what I mean by an institutionalist research program, by describing those particular features that are relevant for the study of technical change. Later sections present more specific propositions concerning investment and innovation.

5.2   INSTITUTIONAL ECONOMICS

In a world of unbounded rationality investment decisions are trivial, in that the optimal decision is obvious. The possible courses of action and the joint probability distribution of the future states of the world that result from these actions are given and known. Within this framework, agents would have to be irrational not to make the choices that maximize expected utility, and such obvious irrationality among economic agents is not plausible, except as a temporary aberration. So neoclassical growth models automatically assume that agents choose the profit-maximizing sequence of investments from the given set of alternatives.

It is important to identify what it is that distinguishes institutionalist reasoning from neoclassical models. The institutionalist approach does not suggest that agents are irrational, but that possible courses of action are not pre-ordained and are not known *ex ante*. There is no given set of well-defined alternatives, and choices made at each step refigure the alternatives that are available. That is, the choice-set changes endogenously. Individuals have to explore, define, learn about possible courses of action, with limited means for doing so. Much of this searching and learning is by doing. As economic agents put their decisions into practice and learn about their environment, a new set of ends and means emerges. In short, as they act, agents change the environment and their own means for dealing with it. Hence they change the courses of action subsequently available to them.

A possible objection is that the search process can be expressed as an optimization problem and adequately treated within neoclassical models. Neoclassical models already provide a precise and formal way of dealing with uncertainty and information issues. To understand the difference between the approaches, consider the neoclassical definition of uncertainty. The individual does not know which state of the world will occur, but is able to represent his beliefs as to the likelihood of different states by a 'subjective' probability distribution. The notion of subjective probability provides the justification for assuming that individuals can always assign an exact numerical probability to each possible state. Given this assumption, Frank Knight's distinction between uncertainty and risk is not meaningful (Hirshleifer and Riley 1992: 8–10). *Subjectively* the probability distribution of future events is always known. Agents' decisions concerning the future can therefore be analyzed in terms of optimization and equilibrium. Since 'probability is simply a *degree of belief*', all that the neoclassical approach to uncertainty requires is 'precise self knowledge' on the part of economic agents (Hirshleifer and Riley 1992: 8, italics in the original). There is no reason to inquire about what agents know and how they have learnt it, as the analysis starts with whatever it is that agents believe.

In fact, this way of dealing with uncertainty relies on another fundamental assumption besides precise self-knowledge. It requires that the choice-set available to the agents be well-defined and given *independently* of the choices made by the agents, so that the choices are optimal on the basis of the given possibilities. This is an assumption not only about the agents' cognitive abilities but more generally about how the world is ordered. Put simply, institutionalism embodies a different view of the world, one in which economically significant situations cannot be assumed to present courses of action and their consequences as ready-made blueprints. This rejection of the given ends and means framework, combined with the recognition that agents have limited cognitive abilities, implies the irrelevance of the basic neoclassical tool of optimization. Once it is accepted that the agent has to search for possible courses of action, a consistent application of the optimization problem leads to an infinite regress of calculation.[7] To optimally estimate the optimum search path, individuals would have to calculate the costs and benefits of the estimation, but prior to that they would have to calculate the costs and benefits of calculating the costs and benefits of estimating the optimal search path, etc. Without the crucial auxiliary assumption that the choice set is given, an attempt to be rational without limits leads to a form of irrationality, an infinite regress of calculation.[8]

Human beings recognize the bounds of calculation and make social arrangements that avoid uncertainty. Since the 'optimal' outcome is a will-o'-the-wisp in many situations, rational human beings do not pursue it. Instead, we develop rules, conventions, etc. to guide decision making. In this way we 'transform intractable decision problems into tractable ones' (Simon 1982 vol. 2: 8.4). By following rules and conventions as to how to behave under certain circumstances, the individual avoids the need to define the set of alternative courses of action and to predict the consequences of each course. An 'institution' is a rule, convention, or organization that persists and is widely recognized.[9] In more pithy and general terms, institutions are 'settled habits of thought common to the generality of men' (Veblen 1919: 239).[10] Institutions serve as 'behavioral guides that reduce the knowledge and cognitive skills necessary for successful action' (Langlois 1986: 217). An institution defines the possible courses of action in a given situation, and hence limits the scope of calculating rationality.

How rules and conventions evolve and how individuals use these to avoid uncertainty are central questions of the institutionalist research program. This application of bounded rationality, which can be implicit or explicit, is the common ground that justifies delineating the work of otherwise diverse authors as part and parcel of the same research program.

Older institutionalists like Veblen and Commons described how institutions function, but did not provide a logical analysis of why and how institutions matter for economic outcomes. A better understanding of the question 'why' started with Herbert Simon's explicit distinction between unbounded and bounded rationality. The behaviorist and evolutionary writings on the firm developed this insight. Veblen and Commons also illustrated that there need be nothing 'optimal' about institutions. In his explanation of the advantages of late industrializer Germany over Britain, Veblen pointed to the economic ossification caused by aging institutions. But he did not explain how wasteful conventions come into being and why they may persist. Recent studies of technological and organizational lock-in provide the basis for a systematic explanation of inefficient but persistent institutional structures (David 1986; Arthur 1989; Cowan 1990; Lazonick 1991, 1992).[11]

By contrast, neoclassical explanations of non-government institutions such as common law and vertical integration in firms have a Panglossian quality. With the exception of the state, institutions are presented as optimal arrangements, and those that are not are expected to disappear. The idea that institutions, with the exception of state-related ones, tend to be efficient in some sense or another, that for example they maximize wealth, can be justified in terms of the 'survival of the fittest' metaphor. Inefficient institutions lose out in competition with efficient institutions. The usual assumptions that underlie neoclassical theorizing lead to this conclusion. One, there is a given set of alternative institutional possibilities. Without this assumption, the question of the origin of an institution would arise, a question that neoclassical models of institutions do not answer. Two, there is a specific feedback mechanism that favors the efficient among the alternatives. As Langlois has shown, this mechanism has to be swift and effective if problems of path dependency are to be avoided (1989, 1988). Implicitly, neoclassical models of institutions assume that there is such a mechanism, without necessarily specifying what exactly it is or why it can be depended on to work quickly and effectively. By contrast, in institutionalist economics the selection mechanism is a subject of investigation. In some cases, an efficient institution may be selected, but that cannot be presumed.[12] The institutionalist research program asks how an institution came into being, why it may or may not persist, whether it promotes growth or decline, innovation or stasis.

The contrast with neoclassical theory may help highlight distinctive features of institutionalist thinking. In the neoclassical program, the individual agent optimizes independently of other agents and the interaction between agents is through market exchange (or at least can be treated as such). Equilibrium is the consistency condition for the exchange relationship. A researcher working within this program follows the guidelines:

- Specify the objective function and the constraints, and describe the optimal choices for the economic agents,
- Find the equilibrium solution(s) (or, in rare cases, show that there is none).

In the institutionalist approach, there is no given objective function and constraints, and hence an 'optimal' choice cannot be defined. Instead, agents establish what they regard as 'satisfactory' targets, and seek to achieve these targets through feedback corrections. Institutions govern the choice of targets and the routes agents take in searching for satisfactory outcomes. The guidelines for the researcher are:

- Specify the outcomes agents regard as satisfactory and explain how these evolve,
- Investigate the institutional patterns that govern behavior in seeking these targets.

Some authors use the word equilibrium to describe persistent institutional structures (North 1990a). There is a superficial similarity in that an institution consists of a regular, repetitive pattern. But the resemblance is misleading, because an institution and an equilibrium embody inconsistent definitions of change. By definition, an equilibrium state does not endogenously generate disruptions: it is a state of consistency that persists as long as there is no exogenous change. In equilibrium each agent's choices are optimal, given the agent's preferences, and are consistent with the choices of all other agents. This state of things can be disrupted by an exogenous change in the data, but does not change endogenously.[13] By contrast, institutions can change endogenously. Furthermore, institutions evolve in historical time and are path-dependent. Hence they cannot be adequately understood independently of their history. Equilibrium is a way of reasoning in notional time, where changes are reversible and the outcome is independent of the path followed. The 'history' of an equilibrium usually has little significance.

5.3   BOUNDED RATIONALITY

To repeat, bounded rationality applies to decision-making under circumstances where the alternatives are not given *ex ante* and are not independent of the decisions made.[14] Under such circumstances, an attempt to predict the best course of action leads to an infinite regress of calculation. Agents try to limit the need for prediction in making decisions. To do so, they use two procedures. One, they follow rules. Two, they use feedback corrections to achieve goals. Agents have a simplified and not necessarily accurate model of their environment.[15] As they acquire additional information about the environment, they modify their model. The model can consist of a list of rules or instructions as to what to do under certain circumstances. In situations where the choices are well-defined and exogenously given, this way of reasoning does not apply.

Simon's metaphor of an individual in a maze is a useful illustration of what bounded rationality means.[16] The maze consists of endless series of branching-off points and there is no *ex ante* knowledge of its shape. Some of the branches of the maze have a meal at the end, others have nothing. The meals vary, and the individual comes to prefer some meals over others. This preference is a function of the individual's previous experience in the maze, and changes with subsequent experiences. As the individual proceeds, some of the branches close off as a result of his choices and consequently the topography of the maze changes. These conditions have the following implications.

1. The determinants of the individual's behavior are path dependent.[17] The choices available to the individual at any one time depend on his location in the maze, which is a function of his past decisions. The rules he follows in making decisions and the goals he pursues are based on his past experience. He acquires information about his environment along the particular route he follows, and constructs a partial model of the maze on the basis of this information. Decision-making rules are based on this model. He sets goals that realistically can be achieved in view of the available information. These are adjusted as the individual acquires new information. The temporal order of the decisions matters, because it alters the information base and the choice set. Path dependency is thus pervasive, and the outcomes can be understood only by studying the process.

2. A single globally optimal goal is not operational, in the sense that the individual does not know how to achieve it and has no criteria to indicate whether he is achieving it. For example, the single goal, 'maximum number of superior meals for given search time', does not indicate what the individual should do to achieve it. If the individual had, *ex ante*, a map of the maze with all the meals marked on it, he could plot a course to achieve this goal. In that case, the assumption of bounded rationality would be inapplicable. But if the choice-set is not defined, neither is the 'best' choice. Instead of pursuing the pipe-dream of 'the best', the individual formulates specific targets and organizes his search to meet these goals. This

procedure does not require a map of the maze, and avoids the need to make predictions. The individual looks for outcomes that are satisfactory in the sense of meeting or exceeding the targets.

3.   The decision-making rules and the model that underlies them reflect the individual's partial knowledge and subjective evaluation of the maze. The individual may come to a part of the maze where the model is misleading, experience a series of dissappointments, and eventually discard the model and the rules based on it. In the meantime, however, he has made decisions that will affect the choices and the information available to him. In short, wrong decisions are just as significant as right decisions in determining the subsequent route.

This model of the agent and the environment is particularly relevant for the study of technical change and investment. The predicament of economic agents making such decisions resembles the circumstances of Simon's maze. The decision-maker does not know future technological possibilities and learns about them over time in a piecemeal way. This learning is a function of past production experience and past decisions about investment and research. Technological outcomes are a function of this cumulative process, and technology can lock into suboptimal configurations such as the well-known QWERTY keyboard. The assumption that investment decisions are boundedly rational leads to a research program focused on the rules and specific targets used in making decisions. If completed, this research program should yield a set of models that economic agents use in making decisions about investment and innovation. The current literature is far from this state of development, but some basic concepts have been established. We will discuss these building blocks.

5.4   THE CAPABILITIES THEORY OF THE FIRM

The conventional view of the firm as a black box, described by a production function, is consistent with the postulate of unbounded rationality, and its necessary condition, a given choice set. From this perspective the relevant outcome is necessarily the optimal one, which can be defined independently of the decision-making process. Non-optimal outcomes are temporary mistakes, corrected in the long run and hence irrelevant. Even when it is concerned with the uncertain future, the optimizing decision is not affected by the process through which it is reached, as long as it is based on a complete set of precise probabilistic predictions. In short, unbounded rational choice is independent of the decision-making process. Therefore a study of decision-making in firms is a waste, if not misleading. By contrast, bounded rationality implies that economic agents' decisions depend on the institutional setting, since the latter defines the choice-set. The specific conventions and rules prevalent in firms influence economic outcomes, and therefore are an important topic for investigation.

In the presence of bounded rationality, the firm plays a significant economic role as a collection of abilities geared to negotiating technological and market 'mazes'. Through experience the firm learns how to do things; how to produce certain commodities, sell in certain markets, do certain types of R&D. It learns how to organize itself so as to achieve these tasks. The firm possesses interrelated rules, ways of doing things, that govern the various activities taking place within its legal framework (Nelson and Winter 1982). These 'routines' reflect the firm's learning experience, that is, its past. Organizational routines make it possible for a group of individuals to systematically pursue and achieve collective goals that they would not be able to reach as individuals. In particular, the routinized knowledge that members of the firm share forms a collective rationality.[18] This makes it possible for the firm to produce more efficiently than if individuals toiled separately and exchanged their products. These learned and partly tacit capabilities 'permit the enterprise to be more than the sum of its parts. They give it a life of its own above and beyond that of the individuals involved. The individuals come and go, the organization remains'. (Chandler 1992: 86)[19]

Capabilities become embedded in the collective human capital of the firm's employees.[20] A single individual possesses only a small fraction of this firm-specific human capital, and can be replaced as long as the remaining employees are able to train others to do that individual's tasks. Some capabilities are tacit and transfer costs are significant.

Firm-specific capabilities have public good characteristics for the firm. Once such knowledge is acquired, there is no limit to the firm's use of it as a template to produce the same product in ever increasing quantities or to produce related products that rely on the same capabilities (or part thereof). As the fixed cost of developing the capabilities is spread over larger quantities and more products, the firm's average cost falls below that of other (or potential) producers who do not have such templates (Lazonick 1991). Thus capabilities are a source of intra-firm increasing returns. In the previous chapter we considered new classical growth models that assume increasing returns to knowledge available to all firms. By contrast, historical studies suggest significant increasing returns within the firm that has the organizational capabilities (Chandler 1990). This helps explain the long-term persistence of oligopolistic market structures in certain industries.

Core capabilities form the basis of the firm's growth. These originate from the firm's initial experience with specific products and markets. Two characteristics identify core capabilities (Prahalad and Hamel 1990).[21]

1. The knowledge is hard to imitate. Imitation is difficult partly because of the tacitness of the knowledge (Nelson and Winter 1982) and partly because the knowledge is not a single piece of information but an entire pattern of procedures and rules. Obviously, knowledge that is easy to imitate could not be a source of competitive advantage for the firm in the long run.

2. At least part of the knowledge is applicable to other products or markets. If it is not, then the firm will not be able to achieve economies of scope.

Chandler's detailed studies of late nineteenth to early twentieth-century American corporations document the importance of economies of scale (1961; 1976).[22] Successful corporations spread the fixed cost of capabilities over long runs of mass-produced standardized products. First movers achieved economies of scale by building market share, and were able to further expand their market share due to their lower average costs. The oligopolistic power acquired in this interaction continued to ward off potential competitors for many decades. Economies of scope, that is, the application of core capabilities to new products and markets, may have become more significant in the twentieth century.

There may be ambiguities in the theoretical definition of 'core capabilities', but the concept is straightforward to apply in practice. Current management literature provides numerous examples, both for the US and other economies. For example, Canon learnt about optics and precision mechanics by manufacturing basic cameras, then applied this knowledge to developing and manufacturing a wide range of products: electronic cameras, video cameras, printers, copiers. The capabilities acquired from the experience of manufacturing and selling cameras became the basis of the firm's growth (Prahalad and Hamel 1990: 90).[23]

The organizational structure of the firm is a crucial part of the story of how firms achieve economies of scale and scope. The multidivisional form made it possible for corporations to expand to new geographical areas and products by decentralizing decision-making. Operating decisions concerning a particular geographical area or product line were delegated to the division managers. Compared to the unidivisional form, the multidivisional form reduced the amount of information going up and down the corporate lines of authority (Williamson 1971). The central office did not have to concern itself with operating details, and instead could focus on strategic decision-making. This organizational structure made it possible to manage increasing numbers of geographical and product divisions. Hence the structure complemented the strategy of building capabilities and achieving economies of scale and scope (Lazonick 1990). The firm's decisions to invest in production, marketing and managerial capabilities made for sustained growth and competitive advantage (Chandler 1990).

From this perspective, investment is the way firms compete in the Schumpeterian process of moving first to learn and create capabilities. The continued success of a firm depends on reconfiguring capabilities for new products and preferences. Schumpeterian competition, as opposed to price competition, is the race to take the lead in shaping the environment in ways that make use of one's core capabilities and to continue adapting capabilities to the changing environment.

5.5 ROUTINES

The firm 'learns' by accumulating procedures for achieving various ends. Procedures are 'remembered' by being used and become routinized through repeated use.[24] Procedures are used at all levels of the organization, and form a hierarchy of routines that matches the organizational hierarchy (Chandler 1992; Nelson and Winter 1982). Lower-order organizational rules such as to how to file a document or how to start the assembly line are simple, automatic, and frequently repeated.[25] Just as driving along an accustomed route does not require deliberation, simple organizational routines require little deliberate choice by the individual employee performing them. The next step at each turn is obvious because the frame of reference for the activity is constant, clearly defined, and familiar to the actor. Modifications in lower-order routines require decision-making higher up in the organizational hierarchy, using more complicated procedures. Procedures used in ordering new computers or restructuring the assembly line are of this sort. Compared to simple routines, which are specific and clear-cut, higher-order procedures require deliberation, are general rather than specific, and are less frequently used.

Routines are adapted to a specific environment and make for smooth functioning in the context of that environment. This ability to function smoothly gives the firm competitive advantage. However, when conditions change, old rules and conventions can become dysfunctional. Furthermore, overhauling routines is costly and uncertain (Loasby 1986). A central problem facing the firm in making investment decisions is how to establish a balance between established patterns of behavior and the need to make changes.

Routines generate organizational conservatism.[26] The following 'conservative' features have a bearing on investment and technical change:

1.   In long-standing organizations, highly routinized activities tend to encroach on relatively less routinized, more deliberate, activities.

The more routinized a task, the simpler it is to perform. Such tasks are also easier to monitor and impose time limits on. Typically, highly routinized tasks are subject to deadlines and to closer monitoring than less routine tasks. Hence employees give priority to performing more routinized rather than less routinized tasks. In an organization where employees have a multitude of tasks to perform, this leads to what March and Simon (1958) have dubbed the 'Gresham's Law' of organization: routine drives out deliberative action.[27]

Organizations avoid 'Gresham's Law' by institutionalizing activities that require deliberation, in particular, search activities. That is, the organization sets up divisions expressly for the purpose of searching for new ways of doing things. Employees with special skills are charged with this task and procedures for searching are established. Long-term corporate strategy includes changes in production or marketing procedures. The prime example of institutionalized search is, of course, the R&D department. But this is only one of several types of institutionalized search; firms also assign personnel to look for new marketing procedures or financial strategies.

2. Higher order routines are harder to change than lower order routines.

Higher-order rules are general and vague rather than specific and clear-cut. Their application is therefore harder to monitor. Inefficiences in such procedures are typically difficult to trace, and even if the root cause of an inefficiency is found, required changes are harder to pinpoint and to monitor. Furthermore, since higher-order procedures are used in the upper echelons of the organization, vested interests that may be hurt by a change have more power to derail it. Hence a modification of managerial decision-making procedures is more uncertain and costlier than, say, a change in the document filing system. Because of this, organizations try to confine changes to the lower end of the spectrum, except under extreme duress (Chandler 1961: 1990 introduction).

3. Long-standing routines are harder to change than those of relatively recent origin. Awareness of an established routine diminishes with time. The users of a new routine are likely to be aware of what it accomplishes and the reasons for using it, because they remember how and why it was started, or at least have heard about its origins. The users of a long-established routine are less likely to know its rationale and origins. Such routines become automatic responses to certain stimuli and come to resemble natural reflexes rather than deliberate human constructions. In time, routines become invisible to their users.[28] The cost of changing a routine grows as it becomes deeply embedded in individuals' behavioral patterns. Simply recognizing the pattern and the possibility of changing it requires more resources than would be the case with a more recently established and hence transparent procedure.

5.6   INVESTMENT POSSIBILITIES

Capabilities shape a firm's investment opportunities in several ways (Chandler 1992: 98). Production and marketing procedures used by operating divisions are complementary to the firm's physical and intangible capital.[29] An automobile manufacturer's procedures for stamping the steel panels of a certain type of car body complements the plants and the patents for such cars. This complementary relationship between operating routines and conventional resources places limits on the firm's investments. If it is to continue exploiting existing routines, the firm has to invest in facilities and other forms of capital that are related to its capabilities. The strategic decision-making rules used by the central office also set bounds on the investment opportunities considered by the firm. These higher-order routines guide the search for and evaluation of investment projects.

It is useful to define a potential investment project as any proposed change in the firm's inputs or outputs.[30] The more closely a project is related to the technologies and markets the firm has experience with, the more existing operating routines can be used in the project. A 'local' project is one that is relatively close to existing practices (Nelson and Winter 1982). We will assume that projects can be ranked according to their 'distance' from the firm's existing capabilities, starting (at the origin) with the most local projects (Figure 5.1).[31]

The inverse function in Figure 5.1 is based on the following assumptions. The firm's project search routines and the technological trajectories that underlie existing products are given.[32] The search procedures are

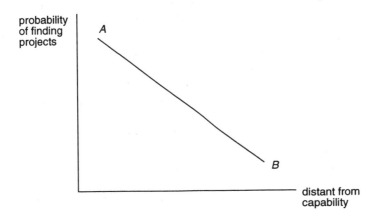

Figure 5.1

geared to existing experience and are therefore more successful in locating opportunities closer to this experience. That is, the firm is more likely to identify projects similar to or related to what it has already done and knows about. Hence there is an inverse relationship between the distance from capabilities and the probability of finding projects using given search procedures. As firms exhaust the possibilities along the given technological trajectory, *AB* shifts down.

Once a project is found and defined, how is it evaluated? In the context of bounded rationality, the key question is what information the firm possesses that can be used for this purpose. The firm knows the *ex post* rates of return on past projects it has undertaken. Surveys of business executives show that the use of historically determined 'hurdle' rates is prevalent across a wide variety of industries (Bromiley 1986; Dertouzos et al. 1989). An average benchmark rate of return, based on the firm's experience, is adjusted for the degree of uncertainty associated with a project. The decision as to whether to undertake the project is based on how it compares to the adjusted benchmark. This procedure does not require an exact estimate of the expected rate of return from the project, only a judgment as whether the project will be more or less profitable than the benchmark. It also does not require information about alternative projects. Hence the amount of information is significantly less than what would be required for an optimizing choice among alternative projects.

The shorter the distance of the project from the firm's current practice, the more information the firm has that is relevant for the project. The more local the project, the less uncertainty the firm faces about it.[33] The premium added to the hurdle rate used to make the decision is a positive function of the uncertainty about the project. Relatively local projects involve less uncertainty and are therefore subject to lower hurdle rates. The result is a positive relationship between the hurdle rate and the distance of the project from the firm's capabilities (Figure 5.2).[34]

The $A'B'$ schedule shows that the firm is willing to undertake a more distant investment only if it subjectively expects a higher rate of return from it. The slope of $A'B'$ indicates the firm's perception of the incremental uncertainty of projects ranked according to distance from existing capabilities. The steeper the slope, the less information the firm has about distant projects. Projects that fall on or above $A'B'$ are 'satisfactory'.

Taken together, the schedules *AB* and $A'B'$ imply that local projects are both more likely to be found and more likely to pass muster. *AB* indicates a larger cluster of projects to the north-west of the graph, and $A'B'$ identifies part of this cluster as satisfactory.[35] For given technological trajectories and search procedures, local projects are more likely to be undertaken than distant projects. As various firms continue to invest in

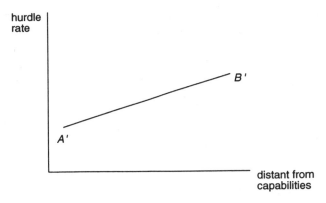

Figure 5.2

similiar projects spawned by the same technological breakthrough, the trajectory is exhausted and *AB* shifts down. The cluster identified as satisfactory by *A'B'* shrinks.[36]

It may be useful to restate the basic difference between this institutionalist story and neoclassical treatments of investment. The approach described here takes the set of possible investment projects as an object of investigation. It starts with the questions: Where do firms look for projects? What procedures do they use in conducting the search for investment possibilities? What determines the chances of finding projects? The choice-set is explained in terms of existing capabilities, including search routines. By contrast, neoclassical models take the set of investment opportunities as given, and describe the optimum outcome assuming there is a well-defined set.

5.7 INVESTMENT STRATEGIES

A firm's investment strategy can be characterized in terms of two types of uncertainty. Productive uncertainty arises from the internal operations of the organization, whereas competitive uncertainty is rooted in the external market environment in which the firm operates (Lazonick 1990: 200). Investment strategies involve a trade-off between these two types of uncertainty. At one extreme, a pure static strategy takes technology and preferences as given. The technology is already in use and its attributes are known, therefore there is relatively little productive uncertainty. But the firm is vulnerable to changes in the market environment brought about by other agents. An innovative strategy, by contrast, aims at changing technology and/or preferences, and hence increases productive uncertainty. In return, a successful innovative strategy enchances the firm's market power and reduces the competitive uncertainty it faces. In short, static strategies involve low productive uncertainty but high competitive uncertainty, while the reverse is the case for innovatives strategies (Lazonick 1990: 205–6).[37]

The experience Chandler describes, of the first-mover firms that remained dominant in their industries for several decades can be understood in terms of these firms' success in reducing competitive uncertainty. The high fixed cost of acquiring production, distribution, management and research capabilities was an effective entry barrier. The entrenched oligopolies, having moved down the learning curve and achieved increasing returns to scale and scope, had the advantage of lower per unit costs. Behind the entry barriers formed by their organizational capabilities, the oligopolistic firms faced little competitive uncertainty for substantial periods of time.

As a technology ages, it tends to become more standardized. Information about it becomes public and the cost of purchasing the know-how necessary to implement it goes down. It becomes possible for firms to purchase organizational and technological know-how ready-made rather than learn by doing. When this happens, entry barriers come down and competitive uncertainty in the product market increases. A firm following a Schumpeterian innovative investment strategy moves to new technologies and markets, erecting entry barriers in the process. A firm following a static strategy stays in (or moves into) markets where the technology and preferences are not changing. Such a firm can buy the standardized managerial and technical know-how from outside suppliers, and does not need to acquire special in-house capabilities. Since the inputs are available to anybody, the static firm faces more uncertainty in its environment. It engages in price competition rather than Schumpeterian competition, and more closely resembles the conventional neoclassical depiction of the firm. A long-term innovative strategy requires that the firm:

- develop a set of core capabilities that are both hard to imitate and flexible enough to be applied in other areas;
- evolve the organizational structure that facilitates a high rate of utilisation of these capabilities;
- increase market share to reap economies of scale;
- find new products related to core capabilities to benefit from economies of scope.

These concepts have real-world counterparts and direct implications for corporate management. The capabilities approach to the firm implies that to be successful, an innovative strategy has to be based on a set of core capabilities (Prahalad and Hamel 1990). Market entry decisions have to take these into account. Diversification decisions have to be based on gaps in capabilities that can be filled by acquiring ready-made skills. The management of human resources has to encourage flexibility in applying existing skills. In particular, achieving economies of scope requires the ability to cut across different divisions to identify hybrid opportunities, such as applying knowledge acquired in the camera division to developing a laser copier. (Prahalad and Hamel 1990: 90). A firm also has to be aware that divesting itself of core capabilities is usually an irreversible decision. For example, when a firm closes off a division and uses outside suppliers instead, the learning process ends and a subset of the firm's capabilities atrophies. The decision to do this should take into account that 'when it comes to core competencies, it is difficult to get off the train, walk to the next station, and reboard' (Prahalad and Hamel 1990: 85).

Historical accounts of technical change show that imbalances and bottlenecks that result from technical progress can in turn act as 'focusing devices' in the continuing search for innovations (Landes 1969; Rosenberg 1976). The search for innovative investment projects may be partially guided by such technological bottlenecks. The idea of focusing devices can perhaps be generalized to technological and institutional barriers that are not necessarily the result of technical change. For example, a stagnant market can be taken as signalling the need for new applications of capabilities.

However, as Parker (1984) and Mokyr (1985 and 1990: 163) have argued, such signals lead to innovation only if the problem cannot be solved by re-allocating resources. In the absence of immobilities, techno-logical bottlenecks can be eased by allocating more resources to that area. A manufacturer in a stagnant market has two broad strategies to choose from. One is to reallocate the firm's capital to existing industries that are more profitable, without attempting to innovate. The other is to invest in new products and/or processes about which there is a higher degree of uncertainty.

For example, consider an automobile manufacturer whose R&D routines date back to the world of low oil prices and gas-guzzling car models. When oil prices rise and consumers switch to fuel-efficient cars, the firm's sales and profits drop. The innovative strategy is to change R&D routines so as to develop fuel-efficient new models. A static allocative response is to move resources to the luxury car market where fuel efficiency is less of an issue, and continue to use existing routines and technologies. Another example is the reaction of major US steel manufacturers to declines in profits due to cheap steel imports. The large steel companies did not attempt to become more competitive by innovating. Instead, they diversified away from steel, acquiring enterprises in unrelated areas such as financial services or car rentals. For the economy at large, this choice meant a lower rate of innovation than would have been the case with the alternative investment strategy. Under what circumstances do firms make innovative investments and under what circumstances do they choose static re-allocation?[38]

One possible variable that could influence such decisions is the transaction cost of acquiring existing businesses. The relative attractiveness of the static allocative strategy partly depends on the cost of acquiring information about and buying shares in other firms. These costs depend on financial institutions and ownership patterns. Information about firms whose shares are frequently traded is more readily available and hence cheaper. In an economy where a predominant number of portfolio holders favor short-run gains over long-period capital appreciation, shares will be traded often and up to date information about most companies will be easy to obtain. This reduces the transaction cost of re-allocating capital, and by conventional arguments promotes static efficiency.

From the point of view of innovation the implications are complicated. If the overall level of investment were taken as constant, the lower transaction cost of re-allocation would encourage static investment strategies. But the more developed capital markets also make it easier to finance all investments, including innovative projects, and are commonly presumed to facilitate a higher level of overall investment. Furthermore, acquisitions of other firms can be part of an innovative strategy that requires the development of new capabilities.[39] Hence the net effect of a highly active stock-market on innovative investment is an open question. Under what conditions would the positive effect on innovative investment be swamped by the negative effect that operates via the greater ease of static re-allocation? Without an analysis of financial variables, which is beyond the scope of this book, it is not possible to go into this issue.[40] It may be that there is some 'optimal' level of development of financial institutions that encourages innovative investment choices. Underdeveloped financial institutions dampen investment, but an overdeveloped financial sector may also discourage innovative investments.[41]

5.8   INNOVATIVE INVESTMENT STRATEGIES AND THE SELECTION ENVIRONMENT

Evolutionary metaphors come in handy in characterizing the interaction between firms and the outside conditions or 'environment' they operate in.

In their evolutionary theory of the firm, Nelson and Winter loosely characterize routines as genes. Mokyr (1990) proposes a slightly different biological metaphor, with technologies as genes. These analogies are suggestive, but a systematic application of biological concepts and models raises possibly intractable issues.[42] Such an application is complicated from the outset by differences of opinion among distinguished biologists. The first question that a serious application of biological analogies to economic phenomena would have to address is which evolutionary model to use and why.[43] Needless to say, these questions are beyond this book.

It is possible to distinguish different kinds of innovative strategies. Certain market and technological conditions favor a first-mover strategy, but a 'fast second' imitator strategy appears to be highly effective under other circumstances (Mowery and Rosenberg 1989: 205–37). That is, a rapid imitator with the ability to learn from the mistakes of the techno-logical pioneer and to make incremental modifications in the product or the process may have advantages over the first mover. There is impres-sionistic evidence that this is the case when the knowledge acquired by the pioneer innovator is not firm-specific and there is rapid technical change after the original innovation. On the other hand, if the pioneer's initial learning is firm-specific, the fast imitation strategy is less likely to be successful. How do firms decide *ex ante* between these two types of innovative strategy, before acquiring the knowledge?

There are two logically distinct, though obviously related, issues here. One is how agents decide which strategy to pursue. What model or rule is used to choose between different innovative strategies? The second issue is the conditions under which a certain rule and the resulting strategy are likely to be successful. In terms of the evolutionary framework, the first issue is concerned with the decision-making routines of firms, the second is about the selection environment. The relationship between the two is a key topic that needs both conceptual and empirical investigation. I can only indicate some of the questions that need to be addressed.

First it should be noted that this use of the evolutionary metaphor is diametrically different from the 'survival of the fittest' type of selection argument employed by some neoclassical authors to justify the use of optimization calculus to describe economic agents.[44] In institutionalist arguments, what traits 'survive' or are 'selected' by a specific environment is the subject of investigation. Also, since the choice-set is not assumed to be given, it is possible that more efficient alternatives are possible, but have not been tried by any agent. Then there is no market mechanism to 'select' such alternatives (Nelson and Winter 1982: 140–1). Hence a key question is how the set of traits is changing. Neoclassical models simply avoid this issue by assuming that the set of relevant alternatives is exogenously given.

What further complicates the relationship between the environment and firms' routines is that the former is not independent of the latter. Parts of the environment may be exogenous, but other features, such as market structure and level of technological know-how, are endogenously determined. The comparative 'fitness', i.e. profitability, of a firm's routines depends on the characteristics of the selection environment, but the latter partly depends on the routines of existing firms. The endogeneity of the environment means that the notion of 'fitness' contributes less to the understanding of the pattern of secular change than might seem to be the case at first glance (Nelson and Winter 1982: 161).

5.9   TECHNOLOGICAL DISCONTINUITIES

Empirical studies have long shown the importance of incremental innovations for productivity growth.[45] These are associated with 'micro inventions' that make for progress along a given technological trajectory (Mokyr 1990; Dosi 1988b). The trajectory is based on a 'technological paradigm' of generic technical knowledge in a particular field. The paradigm specifies general rules, problem solving heuristics, key variables, and ways of pushing back constraints (Nelson 1987: 75). In the course of normal progress problems are defined and solutions found within this frame of reference. Examples of technological paradigms include the internal combustion engine, oil-based synthetic chemistry, and semiconductors (Dosi 1988b: 1127). Commonly, the trajectory of incremental improvements is subject to diminishing returns (Freeman 1986, 1989). Revolutionary shifts in technology bring new paradigms and start new trajectories of incremental improvement, causing discontinuities in normal technical change.

Mokyr points out that normal and revolutionary technical change are complementary. In the absence of new paradigms, incremental progress would peter out as the opportunities presented by the existing paradigm were exhausted. The continuous momentum of modern industrial economies has been due to the emergence of new trajectories from time to time. Conversely, without the stream of microinventions, the economic potential of a technological paradigm could not be realized.[46]

A firm's search routines are adapted to certain paradigms. As the trajectories age, the probability of finding innovative investments falls. (In terms of Figure 5.1, *AB* shifts down.) Existing routines do not necessarily fit the frame of reference of the new technological trajectory. To successfully invest in a new paradigm, a firm may have to modify not just operating routines but higher-order decision-making routines as well. As argued above, higher-order routines are harder to change. One way established firms reduce the uncertainty of such changes is by waiting for entrepreneurial start-up firms to bring about the revolutionary innovations and then acquiring such a business and its established capabilities. The acquiring firm knows what it is getting when it adds the other enterprise's capabilities to its existing stock. However, the long-term success of such a move depends on the ability to accommodate the different routines of the acquisition within the existing organizational structure.

Under these conditions the acquisition of the other firm is part of an innovative strategy of building new capabilities to bridge the discontinuity. The distinction between normal and revolutionary innovations suggests that routine-oriented established corporations and individual entrepreneurs play somewhat different roles in technical change. The former are particularly important in achieving the incremental improvements, while the latter play a pivotal role in bringing about the discontinuous jumps. The Schumpeterian entrepreneur operates outside organizational routines, or if necessary breaks them, and tends to bow out as the radical change is institutionalized. Subsequent incremental improvements are routinized in the organization.

The cost of making changes in higher-order routines depends on the strength of the organizational barriers to such changes. The barriers may include union rules, executives with a vested interest in doing things the old way, legal requirements or threats of lawsuits that add to the cost. A well-known recent example of an attempted change in a long-established enterprise, namely GM's Saturn project, gives a sense of how significant the barriers can be. For the new factory, built at a location far from headquarters, General Motors instituted different training procedures for the workers and managers. The company set up the unit with independent internal decision-making rules and R&D capacity, and negotiated a different agreement with the union. This attempt at a radical break with existing routines came after years of apparently unsuccessful efforts to produce better and lower-cost cars within the existing units. Saturn's independence was thus a protective measure against the forces working against change in the organizational structure. One can surmise that the cost of building the new unit from scratch was less than the cost of changing the routines of existing units.[47]

Evolutionary simulation models delineate the market structures that emerge when firms search and invest according to certain simple rules in a given technological environment. For example, in one model Nelson and

Winter assume a firm's investment is proportional to its excess profits and only firms which achieve a rate of return less than a specified target search for better technologies. They find the simulation results roughly match observed historical trends (1982: 220–1). These models constitute a beginning in dealing explicitly with questions about the nature of search processes undertaken by boundedly rational agents. As Nelson and Winter observe: 'In the simulations the "topography" of new technologies was relatively even over time. However, various studies have shown that often new opportunities open up in clusters' (1982: 229).[48]

At the current stage of development, simulation models have not addressed questions about changes in the selection environment and firm responses to such shifts.

It is likely that most questions about the adaptability of routines to changes in selection criteria are not suitable for analysis at a high level of abstraction. Nelson and Winter draw on the biological literature to identify two traits (or strategies) that make for survival in a varied environment (1982: 161). One is flexibility, the other a high mutation rate. Applied to firms, this implies that firms that possess flexible decision rules and are capable of extensive search activities are favored by a changing environment. This is a plausible hypothesis that can be tested in studies of individual firms.

Empirical and historical studies of the two-way interaction between firm's capabilities and the external environment have already made some progress.[49] Observers have argued that the technological and market environment worldwide has changed in recent decades, and some have argued that certain routines of American firms (at least in some industries) are ill-adapted to these changes. This literature is mostly in the form of case studies and how widely these arguments apply is unclear. The institutionalist framework helps bring coherence to what otherwise appear as ad hoc explanations of conditions in specific industries. The next section highlights the coherence and consistency of these disparate observations within the framework of the capabilities theory of the firm.

5.10   CONVERGENCE VERSUS DIVERGENCE AMONG NATIONAL ECONOMIES

What are the economy-wide implications of the capabilities view of the firm? Consider an economy where most firms were established along technological trajectories that are exhausted at the current period. There have been no major disruptions in the economy and the firms have retained their old organizational structure and decision-making procedures. Historical studies suggest that these firms are unlikely to change their previously successful structure and procedures soon enough to lead the way in exploiting the next round of technological paradigms. Inventions with potentially far-reaching effects may originate in this economy, but are less likely to be successfully exploited by such firms. This may account for the phenomenon Veblen described as the 'penalty' of taking the lead when he compared British and German economic performance in the early twentieth century: 'All this does not mean that the British have sinned against the canons of technology. It is only that they are paying the penalty of having been thrown into the lead and so having shown the way' (1948: 375, first published 1915). The issue brings us to the slippery grounds of the British entrepreneurial failure debate and its successor, the ongoing controversy about American competitiveness.

The story is well known. The British economy, having pioneered early nineteenth-century technologies, was overtaken by Germany, the US, and others who achieved persistently higher productivity growth rates. British firms were late in making the change from the family-oriented unitary form of business organization to the multidivisional form presided over by professional managers.[50] Firms in the latecomer economies organized in a way to take full advantage of the new technologies. Similarly, American firms, the technological and organizational pioneers of the first half of the twentieth century, may now be impeded by their established structure and practices.

What some authors see as US firms (and economy) falling behind, others see as part and parcel of the inevitable process of convergence, whereby Europe and Japan close the gap between their own and US productivity levels.[51] Two points of view can be distinguished in the controversy. The first implies that the US productivity and/or GDP growth rate will remain at a relatively low level after other countries achieve comparable levels of productivity and national income. Historically this has been the case with Britain, where growth continued to be low after other economies caught up. According to the second interpretion, the comparatively high growth rates of other economies will come down to match the lower growth rate of the more mature US economy once the others catch up. The empirical question is beyond the scope of this book (and probably cannot be decided for another decade). The general point that the relative performances of industrial economies may depend on their respective histories provides an example of an institutionalist argument about investment and technical change. The capabilities approach to the firm provides an explanation of how the history of firms limits their possible courses of action in the face of changes in the economic environment, incidentally providing a microeconomic foundation for the 'penalty for taking the lead' argument put forth by Veblen in 1915. Salient features of the environment include the rates at which different technological trajectories are being exploited by firms worldwide and the effect of this on competition in international markets. The issue is how the majority of agents in an economy adapt to the changing international environment and how well firms balance the effectiveness of established routines with the changes required for success in the new environment.

Obviously, if established firms are ill-adapted, other agents can form new companies to exploit the new possibilities. To what extent is that likely?[52] It is relevant to this question that not all of a firm's routines are specific to or developed by that firm. The firm acquires professional rules of conduct and performance evaluation through recruitment:

> When a business firm hires an accountant, a dietician, a doctor, or a sanitary engineer, it hires not only an individual but also a large number of standard operating procedures that have been trained into the new member of the organization by outside agencies. One of the important consequences of professionalization in general is that extraorganizational groups have the responsibility of providing task performance rules for the organization.
>
> (Cyert and March 1963: 105)

These professional rules have the character of public goods, in that their use by one firm does not preclude their use by another.[53] Professionalization means that firms in a national economy share a pool of rules and conventions, in addition to the firm-specific routines. Firms share human capital that has been shaped by (more or less) standardized professional education.[54] Furthermore, members of a profession cooperate in some ways across firm boundaries. Von Hippel (1988) found that engineers working for different firms exchange some types of information and help each other solve technical problems.

Firms also share what are referred to as 'standard industry or business practices'. These economy- or industry-wide informal rules of conduct reduce the uncertainty in an individual firm's environment, insofar as other firms can be assumed to follow the rules. The rules reduce the scope for opportunistic behavior in exchanges between firms and hence reduce transaction costs. The evolution of such agreed-upon common rules of conduct can be thought of as the outcome of a repetitive Prisoners' Dilemma game in which the players remember past plays and outcomes.

In long-established and stable industries agents recognize the advantages of conforming to industry conventions and expect others to do so, on the basis of past experience.

Educational, industrial and professional practices, like the firm's routines, are adapted to specific technological trajectories. The issue of balancing the effectiveness of routinized behavior with sufficient flexibility to adapt to changing circumstances applies to these cross-firm conventions as well as to firm-specific routines. These standards, practices, rules, etc. have characteristics that make for path dependency because they are quasi-irreversible and complementary.[55] Industrial and professional routines are learnt by large numbers of individuals working for different organizations. It is costly for an individual to switch to a new way of doing things. The individuals' human capital and the firms' capabilities are complementary. Change is particularly difficult because it is possible only if a large number of individuals and organizations agree to make the change simultaneously, but there is usually no incentive for a private agent to try to bring about such an agreement.[56] A single firm will not switch because if it does so it will no longer be able to take advantage of the common pool of human capital. Hence educational and professional institutions can become a barrier to adaptation as the environment changes.

The US competitiveness literature is full of examples of quasi-irreversible institutions that different authors accuse of pulling down the performance of American firms. Thus it has been argued that current American finance and accounting practices bias corporate decision-making against long-term innovative investment strategies (Myers 1984: 126–37; Dertouzos et al. 1989: 65–6). Myers (1984) argues that formally correct calculations of discounted cash flow tend to underestimate the highly uncertain 'options value' of R&D. Johnson and Kaplan (1987) argue that accounting data used by American managers has become less relevant for maintaining the coherence of corporate structures. On the workshop level, rigid job descriptions and rules about who does what may have become barriers to successful adaptation to the new environment. Piore and Sabel (1984) have argued that new technological trajectories require different worker skills geared to ensuring a higher level of quality in the product and flexibility in switching from one product line to another.

The MIT team that studied a large sample of manufacturing industries observed two 'obsolete strategies' common to firms in these industries, namely the 'mass production system' and 'parochialism' (Dertouzos et al. 1989: 46–52).[57] The practices that are subsumed under these headings were part of the American success story in the past, and are not easily reversible.

According to the observers, these deeply rooted practices are now preventing the exploitation of new technologies and market conditions.

'Parochialism' indicates a strong domestic orientation, not only in terms of markets but also in the search for new technologies. From the late nineteenth century onward, American corporations were highly successful in producing relatively inexpensive and undifferentiated products for the domestic mass market. The size and homogeneity of this market, unmatched by other national markets, promoted the pioneering practices of American corporations (Chandler 1981; Rosenberg 1972, 1981). In many industries, the firms' strong orientation to the domestic market became entrenched in the twentieth century. Furthermore, a disproportionately high share of commercially successful innovations originated in the US. Corporate R&D departments kept abreast of new technologies with relatively little effort by concentrating on American sources. This search strategy was effective until recent decades. But innovations that originated elsewhere became increasingly more common, while the search procedures of American corporations did not focus on developments abroad.

From the nineteenth to mid-twentieth century, product differentiation in this mass market was superficial and relatively insignificant. Innovation was oriented toward tools and machines for long runs of standard products (Dertouzos et al. 1989; Piore and Sabel 1984). Corporate routines were not adapted to shifting between technologically different products for different market segments or export markets, and did not emphasize product quality. As markets and technologies changed, 'the strength of the earlier mass production system became an obstacle to reorganizing the firm' (Dertouzos et al. 1989: 48). Corporations adapted to the large, unified, monolingual American market now faced competition in the international market. The latter required linguistic and cultural skills as well as the capabilities to design commodities suitable for segmented national markets.

It is beyond this book to judge whether these and other obsolete practices led to the loss of competitive advantage for American firms in some industries. That is an open empirical question that probably can only be answered as the passage of time reveals more of the secular trends. On the basis of the view of the firm presented in this chapter, Veblen's argument that the newcomer unencumbered by obsolete institutions has an advantage is plausible. In a more narrow interpretation, we can say that technological pioneers are unlikely to remain pioneers,[58] because they evolve routines adapted to the earlier environment. The very success of these routines in the earlier period makes them hard to change. Particularly in industries where first-mover advantages matter, pioneers of the earlier technical trajectories tend to be superseded.[59]

Of course, just because an economy is no longer a technological pioneer does not mean that it ceases to experience technical progress and productivity growth. The post-World War II catching-up experience of Europe, Japan and other Asian countries shows the importance of imitation in productivity growth. As noted above, a 'fast second' strategy may be more successful than a first-mover strategy under certain circumstances. However, imitation also requires appropriate capabilities that the former pioneer is unlikely to develop in a hurry. The question of imitation capabilities is also crucial in understanding the experience of underdeveloped economies. The flipside of the coin to convergence among industrial economies is the group of extremely low income countries which seem to be falling further behind. Their experience suggests that 'wrong' institutions can persistently prevent the imitation of the practices necessary for successful exploitation of technologies.

Mowery and Rosenberg explain the success of Japanese firms in commercializing technologies that originated elsewhere as a result of institutions particularly adapted to the fast second strategy (1989: ch. 8). For example, the dominant position of the engineering department and the emphasis on process research made it possible for Japanese corporations to introduce high-quality, lower-cost versions of products and technologies introduced by others (1989: 232). It is not clear how and to what extent the capabilities for developing technologies that originated elsewhere can be used to pursue a first-mover strategy, just as it is not clear how a change in the other direction happens, that is, how former pioneers develop the capabilities for successful imitation. In vew of the increasing globalization of technology (Nelson and Wright 1993), what makes for successful imitation may be more important than what makes for successful pioneering. There are studies that address this question, such as Amsden's (1989) analysis of the characteristics of South Korean firms that made for successful imitation. But a general understanding of the types of routines that result in successful imitation in a given international environment requires more empirical research.

5.11   CONCLUSION

The key concepts of the institutionalist research program need further clarification. The concepts of core capability, routine, distance from existing technology, related products, etc., can be given more substance through empirical application. It is fair to note that this approach has received nothing like the energy and resources that have been devoted to developing Keynesian and neoclassical models, and consequently remains underdeveloped. It has been the contention of this chapter that the conceptual work of Simon, March, Cyert, and Nelson and Winter, together with the historical research done by Chandler, Rosenberg, David, and others, has provided basic building-blocks for an institutionalist theory of investment and technical change. This research agenda poses such questions as: What are the core capabilities of firms in a particular industry? How do they build on these? In what ways are firms changing the environment? How are other firms responding? What constitutes an effective innovative investment strategy in this environment? Under what conditions do the firms make innovative investments instead of re-allocating resources within a given production set? What type of firm structure and routines lead to successful imitation of existing technologies? Clear and full answers to these questions are yet to be provided, but the building blocks exist.

To illustrate how the building blocks can be applied, the appendix to this chapter describes the experience of R&D-based pharmaceutical companies.

APPENDIX

The US pharmaceutical industry is a well-documented case of continuous research and technical change that illustrates the concepts described in this chapter. In effect, firms in this industry operate in two separate, though related, markets, one for patented drugs and the other for drugs not under patent protection (Temin 1981: 60–1). In the first market research-based companies engage in Schumpeterian competition, using new products with patent protection to gain market share. Compared to other manufacturing industries, product innovation is important to an unusual extent in the patented drug market and price competition is exceptionally insignificant (Reuben and Wittcaff 1989: 30).[60] The following discussion is focused on this market. By contrast, the market for drugs not covered by patents is subject to strong price competition from generic producers with no research capabilities.[61]

Characteristics of the Industry

The industry is currently in a state of flux. The following characteristics have been prominent in the post-World War II period.

- The large drug-makers engaging in product competition are highly research intensive. The ratio of R&D to sales was 15 per cent in 1986 for a typical pharmaceutical company, compared to 3.1 per cent for the average large chemical manufacturer (Reuben and Wittcaff 1989: 25), and 1.2 per cent (in 1977) for manufacturing as a whole (Scherer 1992: 46). Relatedly, a comparatively large share of a pharmaceutical company's investment is in intangible capital (Grabowski and Vernon 1981: 11).

- Economies of scale are not important in the manufacturing process (Caves et al. 1991: 8). Production typically is in the form of small-scale batch processes. Physical capital intensity is low by the standards of the rest of the chemical industry.

- Economies of scale and scope are significant in research (Schwartzman 1976: 100) and marketing. Firm capabilities in these areas are discussed in the next section.

- Pharmaceutical companies virtually always seek patent protection. Studies indicate a substantial first-mover advantage. The original patent holder typically acquires brand loyalty after making the product exclusively during the patent life (Comaner 1986: 1189). After the patent expires, generic versions of the drug become available at significantly lower prices than the brand name product. However, the market share of the latter does not erode as much as would be the case in other industries. Caves et al. (1991: 45) estimate that when the ratio of generic price to brand price is 0.456, the market share of all generics is 25.2 per cent.

- The innovator firms inform physicians of new drugs through a variety of promotional activities. In fact, these firms are properly seen as producing information as well as chemical entities. Without information about its safety and effectiveness, a drug cannot be sold in the US. Furthermore, without information about appropriate dosage, frequency of use, side effects, etc., a drug is ineffective. The information that research-based pharmaceutical firms generate is therefore as important as the chemical entity they develop. The relative significance of the information content versus the persuasion component of the promotional activities is an issue.

Typically, a firm's promotion expenditures on a drug decline as the patent expiry date approaches. The total quantity sold of the drug also declines. Apparently the lower generic prices are not sufficient to revive the overall demand for the drug (Caves et al. 1991). The decline in quantity sold can be due to the reduction of advertising by the innovator, or it may be because patents tends to expire at the end of the product cycle, when new substitute drugs have been introduced.[62]

- The overall rate of return in the industry is above average for manufacturing industries. On the other hand, the return on pharmaceutical R&D investment in the 1970s has been estimated at around 9 per cent, which is not significantly different from the returns on investments of comparable risk in other industries (Grabowski 1991: 44–5). Since the 1960s there has been ongoing controversy about the monopoly power of the research-based pharmaceutical companies and the lack of price competition among them. As noted, the prices charged by generic makers is a small fraction of the brand name price (17 per cent as estimated by Caves et al. 1991). The generic makers do no research, and the manufacturing cost is insignificant compared to the cost of R&D. (Manufacturing cost is 7 per cent of the producer's price, by one estimate.) The discounted average cost of a new chemical entity approved for marketing has been estimated as $231 million in 1987 dollars (DiMasi et al. 1991).
- A higher proportion of managers in the research-based firms have a science or engineering background, compared to the rest of the chemical industry, where managers predominantly have business and legal training (Reuben and Wittcaff 1989: 29).

Firm Capabilities

The development of a patentable new pharmaceutical product is a lengthy process consisting of several distinct stages.[63] After the initial decision to start the project, decisions about whether to continue it are made at various stages, as more information becomes available. The initial, informal investigation of a potentially successful chemical entity is significantly cheaper than the human tests that come at the later stages and are required for FDA approval. For this reason, the accuracy of the early decisions to continue a project is a main determinant of the profitability of a research based pharmaceutical firm. The commercial success of R&D projects depends crucially on the procedures used to make such strategic decisions.

    The researchers work in multidisciplinary teams that include a clinician, pharmacologist, and chemist. The transaction costs of hiring new research personnel is high (Wiggins 1981: 69). The chemical entity is typically modified throughout the process. The researcher(s) involved in the initial stage therefore have to be consulted at later stages as well (Schwartzman 1976). This makes it difficult to subcontract part of a research effort focused on a specific chemical entity. Also, uncertainty is so prevalent that the transaction cost of negotiating a contract with an outside researcher acts as a deterrent. As Teece (1980) has argued, under such conditions in-house research facilities are preferable, and this is indeed what one observes in the pharmaceutical industry.

Pharmaceutical firms specialize in certain areas of research. They acquire capabilities in particular therapeutic areas, that is, they focus on a specific group of chemical compounds thought to be effective for certain types of medical conditions. Part of the R&D effort is to develop screening devices for this group of chemicals. 'The screening procedure is a low-cost method of separating compounds that warrant more careful testing from toxic substances and from substances that have no observable pharmacological action.' (Wiggins 1981: 58) An effective screening procedure avoids two types of error. It does not encourage research on chemicals that are unlikely to pass the later tests, and it does not discourage research on chemicals that are likely to pass them.

In the past pharmaceutical companies specialized by developing screening devices for particular areas. The development of screens that can handle many compounds economically was a recurrent problem (Schwartzman 1976: 52). The screening procedures clearly give existing firms competitive advantage in their specialty areas. For example, Hoffman-La Roche developed relatively high quality screens for central nervous system drugs and was successful developing products in this area (Wiggins 1981: 58). Newcomers who lacked screening procedures risked having to perform additional costly research to separate the promising projects from the dead ends.

After a firm conducts the required clinical tests for a new chemical entity, it submits the results to the Food and Drug Administration (FDA). This process of getting FDA approval of the chemical as a marketable drug is notoriously lengthy and complicated. The average duration of R&D for a drug is 12 years; of this, six years are spent in clinical investigation and 2.5 years are needed for the FDA review. Established pharmaceutical firms have procedures for dealing with the FDA regulatory requirements. After lab and animal studies have identified a potentially effective and safe chemical, the company files an application with the FDA to start tests on human beings. These tests start with small-scale, short-run human toxicology studies to determine whether the substance is safe and progress to larger-scale clinical studies to determine whether it is effective against the specified symptoms. The tests become increasingly costly as the substance is used by larger samples of patients. Part of the early decision-making about a project is concerned with the FDA's potential reaction. The FDA can and does reject proposed drugs after all the information from the human tests becomes available. Virtually all chemicals have some toxic side effects and affect different individuals in different ways. The firms watch the FDA's views on specific levels or types of toxicity and degree of effectiveness. It can be said that they accumulate regulatory capabilities.

A promotional activity that is crucial to the success of a new drug is the visits of firm representatives to doctors who are likely to prescribe the drug. These trained 'detail people' form long-term relationships with doctors who work in the therapeutic areas the firm specializes in, and prescribe the types of drugs it produces. This sales force and its relationships with doctors is subject to economies of scale (Wiggins 1981: 65). Once a long-term relationship has been established, a salesperson can present a larger number of related drugs to the same doctor at very low marginal cost. On the other hand, retraining sales people to deal with drugs not related to existing products is a fixed cost and a major consideration in investment decisions.

To summarize, a pharmaceutical firm's R&D capabilities include screening devices to distinguish promising chemical entities from others, procedures for handling regulatory requirements, and a trained sales force with established links to physicians. What the firm produces is information as well as drugs. Marketing capabilities are largely embodied in the sales representitives, who have to be capable of disseminating this information in a way that persuades physicians to use the firm's products. All of these capabilities are fixed costs to the firm. Once the firm acquires these capabilities, it can use them to develop and market any number of drugs, thus creating economies of scope. The economies of scope turn the high fixed costs into low per unit cost per drug, while the ongoing product innovation protects the market power of the oligopolistic firms. The latter's profits are a function of this process, in which large long-term investments in research, regulatory knowledge, and sales capabilities, combined in the right organizational structure, leads to market power and low per unit costs.[64]

This interpretation is confirmed by interviews with pharmaceutical managers, who indicate that one of the main considerations in investment decision-making is 'the project's synergism with existing research and product lines of the company' (Wiggins 1981). A potential new product is evaluated in terms of whether it can be marketed by the existing sales staff, and whether it can be developed in existing research facilities and by existing personnel. A project that requires new facilities and personnel has to promise a higher rate of return. Thus, investment decisions by pharmaceutical firms fit Figure 5.2 very well. Projects that require new capabilities are subject to a higher benchmark. Prior to the changes described in the next section, the firms were likely to find new chemical entities (NCEs) close to their existing capabilities.

A decade ago, interviews with managers indicated a stable R&D expenditures-to-sales ratio in the short run. (Grabowski and Vernon 1981: 5–6) This ratio appears to have been a strategic decision-making routine. It was based on the company's past experience and used to determine the annual R&D budget. These R&D ratios vary between firms but were stable in the 1960s and 70s. More recently, this practice may have changed.

Changes in the Environment

A relatively large number of drugs were introduced in the US market in the immediate post-World War II era, into the early 1960s. There was a marked decline in the number of new drugs per year in the late 1960s and a partial recovery in the 70s. Studies also indicated declining rates of return on phamaceutical R&D from the early 1960s onward (Bailey 1972; Schwartzman 1975). Two different, but not necessarily inconsistent, explanations were offered for these downward trends:

1. Increasing regulatory requirements   The Kefauver Act passed in 1962 gave the FDA greater authority over drug evaluation, and mandated that new drugs be tested not only for toxicity as they had been previously, but also for improved efficacy.[65] The result was the longer, more complicated, and costlier FDA review process, which reduced effective patent life. A number of analysts attribute the lower rate of return to the shorter effective patent life. They argue that R&D expenditures declined (or stopped growing) in response to this, and R&D output, i.e. new drug introductions, followed suit. The FDA processes new drug applications with a substantial lag, which has been a complaint of the industry for decades (Reuben and Wittcaff 1989: 29). New legislation was passed in 1984 as a compromise. The new law made it possible to extend patent life up to five years so as to partially compensate for time lost to the FDA review process.

The review process also has had a more direct and obvious effect on drug introductions. The FDA itself has scarce resources which it allocates among competing applications. It can review and approve only a certain number of new drugs a year. In effect, the FDA's capabilities would have limited new drug introductions even if there were no decline in R&D expenditures. Figure 5.3 shows that the number of new chemical entities approved by the FDA fluctuated from year to year without a clear trend from 1970 to 1988, while pharmaceutical R&D expenditures in real terms stagnated in the 1970s (and more than tripled from 1980 to 1988, a development explained below). More recently the drug industry has been negotiating an agreement with the government according to which the companies will pay fees to help finance additional personnel for the FDA, and thus expedite the review process (Hilts 1992). The companies' willingness to do this indicates their belief that the marginal revenue from a shorter review is greater than the marginal cost of the user fee. This also suggests that the FDA has acted as a bottleneck apart from the effect of regulation on the rate of return and R&D expenditures. Given the rate of return and the current level of R&D expenditures, companies would like to submit more applications than the FDA can handle.

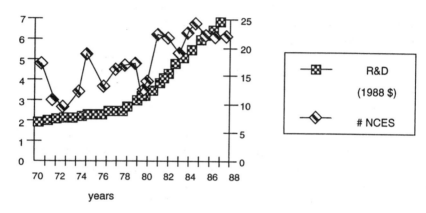

Figure 5.3   FDA approval versus R & D spending
Source: Grabowski 1991: 39. R&D in billions of 1988 dollars.

The 'regulatory excess' explanation of the decline in drug introductions during the 1970s is not consistent with some of the evidence on the subject. The studies that support this explanation rely on regressions run on industry-level data. An analysis of disaggregated classes of drugs presents a different picture. It shows that the decline in introductions is concentrated among certain classes of drugs (Wiggins 1981). These therapeutic classes are not subject to regulations different from those applied to other classes of drugs. So it would appear that there is some other causal factor at work besides regulation.

2.   Declining Research Opportunities   The post-World War II pharmaceutical boom was predominantly based on trial and error rather than exact theoretical understanding of the links between biological processes and chemical entities. By the end of the 1970s the 'try-every-bottle-on-the-shelf approach' had, according to a number of observers, 'gone into the stage of severely diminishing returns' (Scherer 1981: 47).[66] In terms of the concepts developed above, the *AB* schedule (Figure 5.1) had shifted down. The decline in new drug introductions and the return on R&D from the 1960s to the late 70s is at least partially due to this exhaustion of one technological paradigm before the commercial application of the new paradigm became feasible.

As noted above, the rate of return on pharmaceutical R&D investment is estimated to have declined in the 1960s and 70s. But, as Figure 5.3 shows, R&D expenditures remained fairly constant in the 1970s. The continued relatively high R&D expenditures raised the question, Why have drug firms continued to maintain such high levels of investment in R&D if the expected returns are as low as these studies seem to indicate? (Grabowski and Vernon 1981: 17). The framework presented in this chapter offers a plausible explanation:

(i)   As described above, drug companies have specialized capabilities that give them a competitive advantage in developing new drugs. These capabilities are not transferable to R&D in other industries and do not provide a competitive advantage in manufacturing. That is, the research-based oligopolies have no advantage in manufacturing over generic producers with no research capabilities.

(ii) Specialized human capital is necessary to utilize the R&D capabilities. The transaction cost of hiring and firing scientists is high.

These two characteristics imply that existing pharmaceutical firms would not immediately respond to the lower rate of return experienced in the 1960s and 70s. There is some evidence that they tried to adapt existing capabilities to the new environment of increased regulation and declining technological opportunities.

The firms' strategic decision-making procedures did not change in the fifties and sixties. Research scientists (chemists, biologists, clinicians) completely controlled R&D decision-making (Wiggins 1981: 57). Investment decisions were made on the basis of a 'very limited information set' predominantly concerned with scientific feasibility and medical need (Wiggins 1981: 62). But in the seventies managers with business and legal background gained some say in the decisions, and added variables, in particular related to regulatory requirements, to the information set. In short, the likelihood of FDA approval became a major consideration. The project selection process became more formal to include the inputs of managers from different disciplines. The rules of thumb used in making decisions changed. Instead of a total budget determined by the historical R&D-to-sales ratio, sequences of hurdles were increasingly used to evaluate individual projects.

Scientists have to show that a project meets certain criteria at certain dates to assure continued funding of that project.

From the late 1970s onward, the following changes in the environment became prevalent:

1.   Major advances in biomedical science opened up a new technological trajectory. Better understanding of physiological processes at the molecular level and new research tools made it possible to do theory-based pharmaceutical research instead of trial and error experimentation. Random screening of a large number of compounds, which as noted was the predominant method in pharmaceutical research, is giving way to research based on biological models of disease. The emergence of genetics-based biotechnology is part of this shift in the research paradigm.[67] Figure 5.3 shows that pharmaceutical R&D spending (in 1988 prices) increased significantly in the 1980s. The new technological possibilities are the obvious explanation.

2.   Concern with the growth of health-care expenditures led to constraints imposed by third-party payers on prescriptions, such as the formularies used by many states as criteria for Medicaid reimbursement and rules about substitution of generics for brand-name drugs. The spread of managed health care also brings limits on prescriptions. There is impressionistic evidence that the large pharmaceutical manufacturers are developing strategies, such as comparative clinical outcome studies, geared to convincing third-party payers that the benefit of a certain drug exceeds its cost (Telling 1992: 212).

The *research* capabilities of existing firms did not give them a competitive advantage in genetics-based R&D. Consequently, start-up entrepreneurial firms, typically with strong links to university based researchers, have been prevalent in this area. In a study of the relationship between these new biotechnology firms (NBF) and the oligopolistic pharmaceutical manufacturers, Arora and Gamberdella (1990) find that established companies with greater research capabilities are more active in pursuing linkages with NBFs. Arora and Gamberdella argue that the locus of innovation in pharmaceuticals is increasingly the 'network' of relations between the NBFs, universities and the established companies. However, since the industry is in the process of shifting to a new technological trajectory and adjusting to other environmental changes as well, it is likely that the current structure is temporary. Research-intensive established companies are generally following an innovative strategy. Given the uncertainty associated with new technological trajectories, and the 'distance' of this type of research from the existing research capabilities, some established pharmaceutical companies did not initially make investments in the new paradigm but waited for the trajectory to be better established by the NBFs. In time, the established companies following an innovative investment strategy acquired (in part or wholly) the more successful NBFs, or started to build from scratch their own divisions with expertise in genetic research and university ties to such researchers.

Unlike older research capabilities, existing capabilities for dealing with FDA regulations and with the medical profession are relevant for the new technological trajectory. The same regulations apply to the new products and the same doctors have to be informed of these products. Thus the oligopolistic firms can continue to reap economies of scope by using their strategic decision-making routines for marketing and for dealing with regulations. On the basis on the approach outlined here, it would seem that in the long run existing corporations have a potential advantage over NBFs because of these economies of scope. But exploiting this advantage depends on the oligopolies' success in integrating new research capabilities with existing procedures for developing, getting FDA approval for, and commercializing new drugs. Obviously, research is needed to test this scenario.

6 Summing Up

One's approach to investment and technical change depends on how one defines economic agents' rationality. How do agents perceive investment opportunities? How do they form expectations? How do they make choices? The answer a theory gives to these questions is a function of the type of rationality it attributes to decision-makers.

Neoclassical growth theory and some Keynesian growth models are organized around the concept of a steady-state growth path. The two approaches differ in their analysis of the individual agent's decision-making. For post-Keynesians, the investor's expectations are too volatile and unsystematic to be the subject of theoretical inquiry. At a given time, expectations are whatever they happen to be. In the post-Keynesian growth models, the rate of investment depends on a state of given expectations. On the equilibrium growth path, the rate of profit (and the associated functional income distribution) is a function of this rate of investment.

The income distribution thus determined is persistent and relatively steady, but the expectations that determine it are taken to be volatile and arbitrary. This logical inconsistency undermines some versions of post-Keynesian growth theory. Robinson investigates the possibility of steady-state growth, but given her assumption about expectations, the model is indeterminate. A stable equilibrium investment and income distribution configuration is one possibility, but no such configuration or an infinite number of equilibria are equally possible. Mark-up models take as given the rate of growth of product demand expected by the corporation. But the modern corporation that these models claim to represent typically produces more than one product and grows by moving into new markets. Historical studies depict the corporation as an agent that determines the growth of demand, not as one that takes it as data. The institutional structure that the mark-up models assume is at odds with the assumption of a given rate of growth. In general, the various models depicted in Chapter 3 depend on an equilibrium growth rate that is arbitrary, because expectations are arbitrary, and the theory provides no way to go beyond arbitrariness.

By contrast, expectations in neoclassical growth models are consistent with the particular theoretical structure. The theory centers around the concept of equilibrium as a consistency condition of agents' optimizing

123

choices. Agents are unboundedly rational in the sense that all decisions are based on optimizing calculation. This requires that the possible courses of action be exogenously given and well defined. If the choice set is not given, optimization leads to an infinite regress of calculation. The auxiliary assumption of a given choice set is what makes it possible for agents to make optimal choices.

In the context of neoclassical growth models, the choice set includes future production possibilities, which are represented by a production function for technical change. This function can take different forms. An early version is due to the post-Keynesian Kaldor, who postulated a given production function of technical progress. However, this conflicted with his argument that technologies do not exist as ready-to-use blueprints. If that is so, it is even less plausible that technical change exists as a blueprint. A more recent example is Scott (1989), who represents technical change as a relationship between the change in labor input per unit investment and change in output per unit investment. Romer (1990) represents the growth of technical knowledge with a production function that has human capital and the 'stock of knowledge' as its arguments. Whatever the exact formulation, the relationship is exogenously given. In other words, the function and the unit of account of 'knowledge' are independent of technical change. Otherwise, individual agents' choices, including investment decisions, could not be explained in terms of a constrained optimization problem. The behavioral assumption of unbounded rationality does not apply to shifts of the functions, because the shifts violate the necessary auxiliary assumption of a given choice set. Hence theoretical tractability requires that technical change takes place according to a given and stable function. In making technical change an endogenous variable, recent growth models have only succeeded in making it an exogenous function. They have, in effect, substituted the exogenous function for the exogenous rate of technical change assumed by earlier models.

The Marxian accumulation scenario is indeterminate for the same basic reason that modern growth theories conceptualize technical change as an exogenous rate or function. Marx assumes that capitalists will automatically invest a certain fraction of profits. When the profit rate falls, their expectations are disappointed, and the rate of investment declines, causing 'crises'. But in the long run, expectations adjust to the lower rate of profit and capitalists go back to investing the same fraction. This behavioral pattern imputed to capitalists resembles the instinctual activities of ants striving to build an anthill. The Marxian urge to accumulate is socially programmed, and capitalists have little, if any, individual discretion. They follow a given script. But Marx could not help observing that capitalists also act as entrepreneurs who open up new markets and bring out new products. As these developments occur, they collectively increase the proportion of profits invested and shift the economy to a higher growth path. In making such momentous changes, capitalists cannot be following a set program. On the contrary, they are making discretionary choices. A large part of Marx's work relies on the behavioral assumption that capitalists act as socially conditioned automatons. The shifts have to do with a type of behavior that falls beyond this assumption, namely that of the epoch-making entrepreneur. Since such decisions are beyond the scope of Marx's theory, the shifts in the profit rate–growth rate locus are exogenous. They fall beyond Marx's view of capitalists' rationality, just as shifts in the technology production function fall beyond the neoclassical assumption of unbounded rationality.

Classical authors agreed that rational agents prefer more to less. This was a loose and flexible premise that accommodated diverse views of what constitutes 'rational' expectations. Malthusian capitalists exist in a world of chronically deficient aggregate demand, and use a model of this world in making investment decisions. They save a high proportion of their income and, expecting that demand will decline, cut down production. By contrast, Ricardian capitalists have no reason to fear a drop in the demand for their products. If capitalists had repeatedly experienced recessions as described by Malthus, they might indeed have reduced spending and investment, and fulfilled his forecast. But according to Ricardo's reasoning, they could not have had such experience, and hence could not be expected to exhibit the behavior Malthus attributed to them. Malthusian expectations are irrational in a Ricardian world.

Similarly, unbounded rationality becomes irrational in a world where the choices and the possible consequences are not exogenously given and well-defined. If agents have to search for possible courses of action and define the possibilities in the process, optimization falls into an infinite regress. In order to make an optimum decision, the agent has to compare the costs and benefits of the search. But the optimizing agent cannot do that without calculating the costs and benefits of the calculation, and so on and so forth. Furthermore, the agents' search activities can change the possibilities. In Simon's maze, an optimizing individual falls into endless calculation, and hence is irrational.

The institutionalist world is one where individuals define possible courses of action by searching and learning from experience. The lessons from past searches are encoded in stable patterns of behavior recognized by members of an organization or a larger community. Such patterns, whether called norms, conventions or routines, guide the various activities of economic agents. A firm's specific routines give it competitive advantage in certain areas and are a source of increasing returns. Since the choice set is not given but learnt from experience, the agents' past decisions set limits on possible courses of action. Firms search for new projects and evaluate them according to existing routines. The likelihood is high that they will find and choose projects that are close to what they already do.

The activities of firms, as well as public agencies and other agents, change the economic environment. Such changes cause obsolescence in organizational routines. Part of the institutionalist research agenda is about how the environment is changing and what types of behavioral patterns fit the new environment. Part of it is about how firms and national economies adapt to changes in the environment. A key question is to what extent routines formed in previous periods hamper adaptation to the new circumstances.

6.2   WHERE DO WE STAND?

Which approach is more useful? How should the relationship between investment and technical change be studied?

The different assumptions about rationality that underlie the three approaches are appropriate in dealing with different questions. The Keynesian approach does not generalize well to secular growth, because the arbitrary and volatile expectations are more suitable for Keynes's original purpose, namely to account for cyclical fluctuations. The neoclassical approach is appropriate for conditions where the choices and their pay-offs are given and clearly defined, and where there are no endogenous changes in the choice set, constraints, or the pay-offs. That is why neoclassical growth models represent technical change either as an exogenous rate or as an exogenous function.

The behavioral assumption of optimization makes a high level of generality possible. If economic agents optimize under all circumstances and at all times, it is possible, for example, to determine the steady-state growth rate (in terms of given parameters) in the abstract, without inquiring into the specifics of time or place. Thus neoclassical growth models claim general applicability. By contrast, the institutionalist approach to technical change and investment is historically specific.[1] The capabilities theory of the firm is about the modern corporation, an institution that is specific to the late nineteenth and twentieth centuries.

Institutionalism is a heuristic that tells researchers what questions to ask and how to go about answering them. But it does not provide generally applicable answers. The guidelines are general, but the answers vary with the topic, time, and place.[2] As H. Simon has argued, human behavior is not history-free, because human beings learn in time. The learning process results in historical irreversibilities (Simon 1982, vol. 2: 470–1). To really understand why economic agents behave in a certain way, it is necessary to look at their learning process – and that process is specific to time and place.[3]

Unlike the post-Keynesian approach, institutionalism makes it possible to understand the expectations that underlie investment decisions. Unlike neoclassical growth models, it does not impose arbitrary restrictions on technical change. But it does not have the same level of abstraction and generality. Some no doubt consider this a drawback. It would seem that theories of growth face a trade-off between generality and relevance. Neoclassical models sacrifice the relevance; institutionalist explanations sacrifice the generality.

Notes

CHAPTER 1: INTRODUCTION

1. Smith's information about China, based on the reports of visitors and missionaries, was not necessarily accurate. The point made here is not about eighteenth-century China *per se* but Adam Smith's view of growth and capital accumulation. See Rosenberg 1960 for an analysis of the role of institutions in Smith's work.
2. In addition to pp. 111–12, see the references in 111 n.32 (Smith 1776; 1976 edition).
3. Rosenberg and Birdzell 1986 is a historical overview of Western economic growth, with some institutional comparison of other parts of the world. Mokyr 1990 discusses the lack of technical change in China.
4. See Denison 1985 and 1962 for studies of US growth from the growth accounting point of view and Nelson 1973 for an analysis of the weaknesses of growth accounting.
5. See the *Journal of Economic Perspectives* symposium on the productivity slowdown (1988 Fall). Among the contributors Boskin (1988) in particular notes the two-way interaction between investment and innovation.
6. The data compiled according to this definition are published in the *Survey of Current Business*.
7. The two distinctions define four categories of investment: a flow equal to saving; a flow determined independently of saving; a rate equal to the saving propensity; a rate determined independently of the saving propensity. The difference between the first two is not useful for this book, so I have subsumed the two flow definitions under one category in the text.
8. Marglin (1987) notes that there are three views of investment, the short period, the longer period where accumulation is a function of the savings propensity, and the 'asymptotic future beyond all future' of the 1950s–60s vintage neoclassical growth models, where accumulation is determined by exogenous population growth and technical change (986). Marglin's first two categories correspond to the first two concepts I have distinguished in the text. His third category is not so much a definition of investment as a condition of steady-state growth.
9. This issue comes up in Chapter 3, where post-Keynesian growth models are discussed.
10. I use the expressions 'capital accumulation', 'capital formation' and 'investment rate' as synonyms in this book. Throughout the chapters, the 'rate' of accumulation or of investment means the ratio of investment to capital stock. How the conceptual distinctions apply to various models is indicated in the appropriate chapters.
11. See Lund 1971 for a survey of these studies.
12. For surveys of the micro literature on technical change, see Nelson and Winter 1977; Dosi 1988b.

13. This is Arrow's definition of uncertainty (Arrow 1974: 33). Langlois (1989: 227–9) discusses this view of rationality and counter-arguments.
14. Simon also uses the terms substantive and procedural rationality to denote what is referred to in this book as unbounded and bounded rationality (e.g. Simon 1982 vol. 2: 401). For consistency and clarity, I will stick to the latter terminology.
15. Marx can be considered a classical economist (or at least a follower of Ricardo), on the basis of the value and distribution theory he took from Ricardo. See Garegnani 1984 for the features of the classical theory that are common to Marx and other classical authors. Hollander 1979 presents a different view.

CHAPTER 2: THE CLASSICS: DIVERSE BEHAVIOURAL ASSUMPTIONS

1. His argument is based on given (or relatively stagnant) agricultural productivity, given subsistence real wage, and, of course, the fixed supply of land. For a formal interpretation of Ricardo's model, see Pasinetti 1974. For a different interpretation, see Hollander 1979 and Peach 1993.
2. This argument has been formalized by Costabile and Rowthorn 1985.
3. These models are discussed in Chapter 3.
4. Critics of the later post-Keynesian version of the relationship between demand and the profit rate also regard it as a 'temporary' mechanism. This relationship and the debate about it are explained in the next chapter.
5. For Malthus's specific historical examples, see Kurdas 1993.
6. Ricardo had shown that, *ceteris paribus*, there is an inverse relationship between the wage rate and the profit rate. Malthus accepted this result (1963: 189). A modern restatement of Ricardo's reasoning is in Sraffa (1960). The inverse relationship is the centrepiece of what has been proposed as the neo-Ricardian alternative to neoclassical price theory. See Garegnani 1984.
7. This interpretation of the Malthus–Ricardo controversy is inspired by H. Simon's writings on rationality, which are discussed in Chapter 5.
8. See Laibman 1992b for modern treatments of the falling rate of profit argument. Laibman 1987 is a succinct and illuminating treatment of the logic of Marx's argument.
9. Marx's definition of exploitation, the key to his analysis of capitalism, depends on viewing profits as a form of surplus value, that is, not necessary for the reproduction of the economy.
10. See Marx 1954: 555. Other statements on this topic can be found in Marx's attack on the abstinence theory of profits, vol. I, chapter XXIV, section 3. Also see Marx 1963, 1944 Manuscripts (178–80) for a strong statement of Marx's view that accumulation is an end in itself for capitalists and the related point that consumption beyond a given level is not an object. Consumption, Marx argues, is the sign of status in aristocratic society and its remnants, but not for individuals imbued with a capitalist ethic. For the latter, the value of one's assets is more important, and this fuels the need to continue accumulation.

11. Since the difference between surplus value and profit does not matter for the present argument, I will use the terms interchangeably.
12. This argument is in volume III of *Capital* (Marx 1967). On the motivating effect of the profit rate, see p. 259.
13. By Marx's definition, if they cease to accumulate the society they belong to is no longer the 'ism' of capital. It is a different society with different 'laws of motion', not those that Marx is elucidating. See Heilbroner 1985 and 1980.
14. To be more precise, these determine a center of gravity or average rate of return around which actual profit rates fluctuate.
15. This issue reappears in different guises in the coming chapters, and is a central theme of this book.
16. Admittedly, this stretches Marx's meaning: he may have meant an absolute standard of consumption rather than a ratio of consumption to income.
17. Modern scenarios inspired by the Marxian class-struggle scheme also do not ask such questions. See, for example, Gordon, Weisskopf and Bowles 1986.

CHAPTER 3: KEYNES AND THE POST-KEYNESIANS: ARBITRARY EXPECTATIONS

1. Also see Asimakopulos 1990: 335–6.
2. Keynes's version of the marginalist determination of investment is not the same as what later economists considered to be the neoclassical theory of capital accumulation. Jorgenson describes the MEC schedule as 'naive' (Jorgenson 1969: 210). Neoclassical models are the subject of the next chapter.
3. The problem was first pointed out by Hayek in 1932 in relation to the investment function Keynes used in the *Treatise on Money*, but applies with equal force to the MEC formula in the *General Theory*. I owe this point to Raymond Majewski; see Majewski 1988. Garegnani (1982 and 1987a) makes the same point against Pasinetti's (1974) interpretation of the MEC formula. See Mongiovi (1988: 166) for more references.
4. Here Keynes does not explicitly distinguish the choice of technique question from the change of technology question. Capital intensity reflects both of these influences. Nevertheless it is clear that he is describing a conventional neoclassical view of investment in the long run.
5. s/v is the savings per unit of capital. Investment per unit capital has to be equal to this ratio for dynamic macro equilibrium. Obviously, Harrod assumed that s and v are constant. The warranted rate is discussed further in the next section of this chapter. Sen (1970) provides a clear and incisive analysis of the questions raised by this formulation.
6. She developed the approach together with Nicholas Kaldor, whose growth model is discussed later in this chapter. Other economists associated with this approach to growth include Luigi Pasinetti (1974), Jan Kregel (1975), Donald Harris (1978) and the numerous authors cited in the rest of this chapter. There is a distinction between American post-Keynesians, like

Minsky (1975, 1982), who emphasize Keynes's monetary theory, and the Cambridge theorists led by Robinson and Kaldor, who worked on the long-run implications of Keynesian demand-side determination. Furthermore, there is another related group, the neo-Ricardians, who follow Sraffa and concentrate on price theory (see Garegnani 1984). Monetary theory and price theory are beyond the scope of this book. Where there are relevant issues, I will cite the authors without attempting to distinguish which group they belong to within the general post-Keynesian approach. See Milberg 1992 for a description of Eichner's efforts to unify the different groups as one non-neoclassical school of thought.

7. See Loasby 1991 for a discussion of Joan Robinson's research program from a methodological point of view. Robinson saw herself as having taken a wrong turn when she chose to stay within the static Marshallian framework. The failure of the growth model that is the topic of this section is also partly due to this 'wrong turn'.

8. The neoclassical synthesis blurs this distinction between Keynesian and neoclassical models, by making both investment and savings functions of the interest rate.

9. The Harrod model is briefly described in the previous section.

10. There is a huge literature on possible assumptions of different savings propensities from wages and profits. See Jones (1976) for references.

11. Kaldor points out that this mechanism works within limits. See Thirlwall (1987: chapter 6) for a detailed discussion.

12. It should be noted that rate of profit can also increase due to capacity utilization in a short-run conventional Keynesian model. The distributional mechanism in the growth model is different in that it involves a change in the long-run profit rate, not a temporary variation. Vianello (1985) and Garegnani (1992) point out this distinction and argue that changes in investment have no effect on long-term income distribution.

13. See Kurdas (1991) for a discussion of the typology of 'ages'.

14. The participants in this debate do not explicitly address this particular implication, but it is implicit in their argument. See in particular Garegnani 1992.

15. One of Kaldor's 'stylized facts', which are the starting point for growth theorists, is the stability of income shares. The stylized facts are discussed in the next chapter.

16. Again, the critics do not state this explicitly, but it is implicit in their writings.

17. Some economists have claimed that Kalecki has priority of publication (by three years) over Keynes in explicating the dependence of output and employment on effective demand. See Sawyer (1985) for a comprehensive overview of Kalecki's work. Chapter 9 discusses the differences and similarities between the macroeconomics of Keynes and Kalecki, and the claims for Kalecki's priority.

18. Certain other aspects of the investment function are also ignored in this account, such as the distinction between investment decisions and expenditures, because these have no bearing on the point made here. For the general approach to business cycles, see the essays in Kalecki 1969 and 1971 and Sawyer 1985.

19. The following discussion relies heavily on the essays 'Determinants of Investment' and 'Trend and Business Cycle' in Kalecki 1971 and chapters 14–15 in Kalecki 1969.

20. Sawyer (1985) argues that this is indeed the case in Kalecki's treatment of cycles and growth, but acknowledges that innovation remains exogenous (68).

21. In addition to original sources cited in the text, see Thirlwall 1987, chapter 6, for an account of Kaldor's growth model. See Milberg and Elmslie 1992 for a recent synthesis of Kaldor's technical progress function with other post-Keynesian ideas, and Kurz 1991 for a different formalization of the relationship between distribution and growth.

22. See Dosi 1988a for a discussion and more references.

23. Kaldor's empirical work on growth, in particular the so-called Verdoorn's law of dynamic increasing returns, is also part of this approach to technical change (Thirlwall 1987: ch. 7). However, I will not deal with it here, because the empirical (mainly econometric) issues raised by it are beyond the scope of this book. See Gordon (1991) for a critique of the empirical relationship between the rates of growth of productivity and output.

24. A more recent version of post-Keynesian growth theory is presented by Rymes (1989), who integrates the interaction between investment and technical change and the widow's cruse distributional mechanism. Investment in this model is a function of autonomous technical change and the 'growth of primary inputs such as labor and waiting' (663), in addition to the rate of profit. Induced technical change is a function of the rate of accumulation. This model has several shortcomings. Probably the most serious of these is Rymes's use of total factor productivity. Total factor productivity is defined, as in the growth accounting literature, as the residual left after the marginal contribution of each factor is deducted from total output. These marginal contributions are defined as factor shares in output on the basis of marginal productivity theory. Rymes notes this (675 n4) without mentioning that the post-Keynesian widow's cruse story is an alternative to marginalist distribution theory. So the models are two seemingly incompatible explanations for share of profit, namely the marginal product of capital and the rate of accumulation of capital.

25. See Kaldor and Mirrless 1962 where the technical progress function is redefined as a relationship between the rate of growth of output per worker on newly installed equipment and the rate of change of gross fixed investment per worker. This does not make a difference for the outcome of the model.

26. Kaldor does not state this, but it is implicit in the model.

27. See Thirlwall 1987 for a survey of Kaldor's other contributions to the study of growth and development.

28. The acknowledged common ground between Kaldor and the new classical models is their starting point in the 'stylized facts' of growth. These empirical generalizations proposed by Kaldor have been used to justify steady-state growth models, including the recent ones. The stylized facts are discussed in the next chapter.

29. Edward Nell pointed out the relevance of these models for the present discussion of post-Keynesian growth models.

30.   The mark-up pricing literature, which is also referred to as the theory of the managerial firm, includes Marris 1964; Steindl 1976; Wood 1975; Eichner 1976; Nell 1988, 1989a; 92a; Harcourt 1982; Levine 1981. More recent contributions include Canterbery 1992.

31.   These concepts are discussed in the next chapter.

32.   The transaction cost explanation of corporate integration is due to Williamson (1985).

33.   Empirically, this seems to be more applicable to American businesses than, say, Japanese businesses. See Baumol, Blackman and Wolff 1989.

34.   From this point of view, the institutional differences between countries in the relationship between banks and corporations may explain the national differences in the role of internal finance mentioned in the previous note.

35.   Edward Nell brought this implication to my attention.

36.   The impasse is explained above in the section on J. Robinson's growth model.

37.   See, for example, Eckaus 1969 for a discussion of the accelerator.

38.   One attempt to analyze this relationship on a sectoral level is Pasinetti 1981 (71–9). See Milberg and Elmslie 1992 (110–11) for a summary of post-Keynesian thinking on the interaction of demand with technical change, and Nell 1992b for a critical discussion of some post-Keynesian reasoning on the growth of demand.

39.   The relationship of the price to demand on the one hand and to internally generated funds on the other can be thought of in terms of expected quantities (Harcourt 1982) or in terms of growth rates (Levine 1981; Shapiro 1981). The price affects the level of output the firm expects to produce and the internal funds available for investment, all else being equal. These effects can also be seen in the future growth rate of sales and the growth rate of internal funds. Since the focus is on growth in this book, the growth rate version of the mark-up model is presented.

40.   This particular version is from Canterbery 1992: 95, minus the subscripts which are not particularly useful in the present context.

41.   Eichner (1976; 1980) assumes price leadership but also suggests other oligopoly models. Alternatively, the equilibrium price determined by the two functions has been described as a 'strategic price' (Wood 1975) or an industry benchmark that guides the pricing decisions of firms in the industry (Nell 1989b). It is thus not an observed price but a rational expectation based on the market growth and capital formation functions. I am indebted to Raymond Majewski for a comparison of how different mark-up models deal with the question of oligopolistic responses.

42.   As noted above, Wood in particular is aware of this shortcoming of mark-up models. However, it receives little attention in most of the literature.

43.   Cyclical changes in output are not addressed here as they make no difference for this criticism.

44.   The range of products produced by a corporation tend to be related to one another in the sense that they use some common resource. Each business entity has a specific technological base and managerial skills geared to certain markets or technologies (Nelson and Winter 1982). The firm is at a competitive disadvantage with respect to unrelated products that do not use existing technical and managerial skills. Baby-food manufacturers do not

move into the manufacture of space equipment, but may diversify into other baby products or food products for adults. This view of the firm is discussed in Chapter 5.

45. Eichner (1976: 122) seems to think this ability is a characteristic of the conglomerate. Chandler's histories of corporations show that diversification to *related* products is common practice. See the previous note. In retrospect, the 1960s wave of comglomerate diversification into *unrelated* areas appears to have been unsuccessful (1992 Introduction to Chandler 1962).

46. The evolutionary approach is discussed in Chapter 5.

47. See Kurdas 1992 for a description of a possible path of capital formation along the product life cycle.

48. The main reference used in this section is Marglin and Bhaduri 1991. Marglin, 1987 and 1984, also has suggestions along similar lines. Relatedly, a useful graphical comparison of a Keynesian 'growth regime' with other scenarios is Kurz 1991. Another hybrid attempt to integrate the classical Marxian view of investment with more recent ideas is Gordon, Weisskopf and Bowles 1986.

49. The trade-off between the wage rate and the profit rate is with a given technology and given rate of capacity utilization. For a detailed technical exposition of possible interactions between the real wage rate, capacity utilization, and the rate of capital accumulation, see Kurz 1991.

50. This function has a cost of capital variable in it, but Marglin and Bhaduri argue that it can be left out because the goal is to explain the post-war 'golden age' and its demise, and the real interest rate exhibits very little trend during this period, and hovers near zero (1991: 134–5). It therefore cannot explain long-term changes in investment during this time.

CHAPTER 4: NEOCLASSICAL MODELS: UNBOUNDED RATIONALITY

1. See Jorgenson 1963 and 1969 for an original statement of the neoclassical theory of investment. For an overview, see Lund 1971. For a simple summary, see Dornbusch and Fischer 1990 (309–16).

2. See Jones 1976, ch. 7 for a standard exposition, Burmeister and Dobell 1970 for a more detailed and technical presentation.

3. Schmookler could have made the same comment on the premise of exogenous technical change. His path-breaking analysis of patent statistics showed the existence of one kind of endogeneity, namely that innovations can be induced by the growth of demand in the user industries (1966). For a critical review of this hypothesis, see Rosenberg 1982, ch. 10.

4. See Jones 1976 ch. 8 for references, both for vintage models and the invention possibility frontier.

5. See previous note.

6. The conceptual similarity of the models and the growth accounts is worth noting. The 'residual' that remains after the various factor contributions are subtracted can be interpreted as the measure of technical change only if the latter is assumed to be independent of the factor contributions. It is curious

that while the assumption of exogenous technical change was generally considered a weakness of the early growth models, criticism of growth-accounting along these lines, for example, by Abramovitz 1989 and Nelson 1973, 1981, was not widely acknowledged.

7.   The original growth models are described as 'neoclassical' but the new crop goes under the rubric 'new classical', perhaps implying a closer association with the new classical business-cycle models and the rational expectations hypothesis. If there is such a distinction, it does not matter as far as this book is concerned.

8.   For a rich discussion of various interactions, see Abramovitz (1989).

9.   The differences of Scott's definitions from the conventional ones is a large part of his critique of growth accounting and the old neoclassical models. A discussion of these differences in definition is beyond the scope of the present book.

10. Another way of dealing with the uncertainty issue is to simply assume that agents know the probability distribution of returns from all investment projects and have 'rational' expectations. However, if the investment opportunities set is unstable, this assumption will be unrealistic. Again, the stability of the set is the central issue.

11. The models (Romer 1986,1989,1990) are variants on the same idea of endogenous technical change with externalities. My discussion focuses on Romer 1990, which appears to be a more complete formulation of the idea. As is the case in the other sections, only the directly relevant parts of the model are discussed here.

12. Incremental changes in real world technologies have been shown to make significant contributions to productivity growth, for example by Hollander (1965). But even incremental changes are not necessarily 'neutral' with respect to functions and parameters.

13. See Eatwell and Milgate 1983 for references.

14. Actually more than one polio vaccine was developed, but the point made here is nevertheless valid: pre-vaccine treatments were more numerous and would therefore have required more 'designs'. The vaccines caused a revolutionary shift from treatment to prevention, and hence changes the unit of account for technology in this area.

15. For a discussion of the role the stylized facts played in Kaldor's theorizing, see Thirlwall 1987: 173–4.

16. Table 2-4 in Romer 1989, presenting data from Maddison 1987. For US data see *The Economic Report of the President*, 1990.

17. With a very slight upward slope that does not show on the graph.

18. See J. Williamson 1991 for a discussion of Baumol, Blackman and Wolff 1989 (BBW). Williamson points out that BBW, in their zeal to deliver an optimistic message, shift the focus away from certain questions. Williamson finds some of their conclusions questionable. For example, BBW argue that American productivity growth has been lagging for a century, but Williamson thinks the lag is a strictly post-World War II event (J. Williamson 1991: 57–8)

19. A systematic explanation is provided by Lazonick (1991) of the change in economic leadership from the UK to the US and from the latter to Japan. See the next chapter.

20. The study may be less than robust because of the unreliability of nineteenth-century data. nevertheless, the general point that a shift took place in the US economy seems to be accepted by commentators. See Denison's comments on the David article (1977).

21. This hypothesis about saving makes no difference for the argument of this book.

22. David's own use of the comparative equilibrium framework in this paper can be justified as necessary to show the weakness of this framework, but it imposes a certain structure and set of assumptions on shaky data.

CHAPTER 5: NEO-INSTITUTIONALISM: BOUNDED RATIONALITY

1. Simon uses the term 'hyperationality' and notes the dependence of neo-classical theory on auxiliary assumptions that make possible this approach to rationality. Arrow (1974: 28–9, 39–40) sounds the themes of irreversibility and the limits of calculativeness. Elster (1989, 1990) probes the limits of rationality. But neither he nor Arrow advocates an institutionalist perspective on investment and technical change.

2. The term is from Langlois 1986a, but there are differences in definition referred to below. I use 'neo-institutionalism' for brevity.

3. Nelson and Winter (1982) is the main source for evolutionary economics. The behaviorists, in the sense used here, include Simon (1957 and other references in Bibliography), March and Simon (1958); Cyert and March (1963). For the basic tenets of Schumpeterian economics, see Scherer (1984), as well as Nelson and Winter (1982). David (1986, 1989) proposes the description, 'the new microeconomics of technical change' for a large literature that includes Abramovitz (1989), David (1985), Dosi (1982 and other references in Bibliography), Freeman (1986, 1989), Mowery and Rosenberg (1989), Nelson (1987, 1988, 1991 and other references in Bibliography), Teece (1980, 1986, 1988), Rosenberg (1976 and other references in Bibliography). Chandler's (1961, 1977, 1990) research in business history provides much of the material for the institutionalist view of the firm presented in this chapter, which also relies on the development of Chandler's view of the firm by Lazonick (1991). The transaction cost analysis developed by Williamson (1985) is also part of this development. See Langlois (1986a, 1986b, 1989) and Mirowski (1986, 1988) for general methodological discussions of institutionalism. Hodgson (1988) is an in-depth evaluation of the differences between the neoclassical and institutionalist research paradigms.

4. For a commentary from the 'old' institutionalist camp on the new evolutionary economics, see Mirowski (1988). Mirowski is critical of Nelson and Winter's (1982) simulation models, but recognizes their work as part of the 'evolution' of institutional economics. Langlois (1989) chooses to reject the 'old' institutionalism in the name of the 'new', but makes an exception for Commons. For an incisive survey of the latter's main contributions see Biddle (1990). Rutherford (1989) points to the elements of the 'old' institutionalism necessary for an adequate understanding of institutions. Rutherford's objec-

tions to the new institutionalism do not apply to the position presented in this chapter, which is consistent with those elements of the 'old', in particular with the latter's focus on institutional failures. Examples of applied institutionalist writing consistent with the 'old' institutionalism but illustrating the new direction are cited in sections 5. 4 to 5. 10 of this chapter.

5. As examples of the 'old' institutionalist focus on corporate power, see Dugger (1991) and Munkirs (1985).

6. Posner's work is an example of a neoclassical treatment of institutions.

7. In addition to his various writings (in particular Simon 1957 chs. 14, 15), Simon also makes this point in a short story (Simon 1991: 179–88).

8. Simon (1984: 37) has pointed out that neoclassical models (implicitly or explicitly) make auxiliary assumptions to justify the assumption of unbounded rationality.

9. In sociological terms, 'All human activity is subject to habitualization.... Habitualization carries with it the important psychological gain that choices are narrowed' (Berger and Luckmann 1967: 53–4). Institutions are formed when 'habitual action' is recognized by other agents.

10. Presumably also common to the generality of women. Veblen was mostly a man of his own time in his attitudes toward women. For an intellectual biography of this otherwise unconventional thinker, see Dorfman 1934 (1972 edition).

11. One feature that makes for persistence is complementarities between institutions. The formal system of property rights, for example, is complemented by the informal moral principle that stealing is bad. If the majority of individuals in a society do not adhere to the moral stricture, the legal system of property rights becomes non-operational, as enforcement costs become too high. From the experience of numerous underdeveloped countries, it seems complementary institutions that constrain productivity can be extremely persistent.

12. In particular, given the 'wrong' institutions economies become stuck at low levels of productivity, i.e. remain undeveloped. For example, institutions can encourage spoil-seeking instead of productivity-enchancing activities. (North 1990a)

13. An equilibrium may or may not be steady, but the displacement that leads to convergence or divergence is exogenous.

14. The concept of bounded rationality has been used in somewhat different ways by different authors. In particular, Oliver Williamson uses bounded rationality in conjunction with optimal choice of institutions. In this hybrid approach the limited capacity of economic agents to acquire and process information, together with opportunism, gives rise to transaction costs. Optimal institutions minimize transaction costs. Other writers reject the presumption that economic institutions are generally optimal (North 1990 a, b) See Lazonick (1990) for a critique of Williamson's approach. This section relies on Simon's discussion of bounded rationality.

15. The firm may have several different models (Loasby 1986). Loasby analyses such models as Kuhnian paradigms or Lakatosian research programs. This makes it possible to distinguish the firm's acquisition of knowledge about the environment using a given model from changes in the environment that cause revolutionary changes in the firm.

16. Simon refers to the maze in numerous publications (see Bibliography). The discussion here draws in particular on Simon 1957, ch. 15.

17. David (1985) is the classic historical example of path dependency. Cowan (1990) explicitly and Noble (1984) implicitly provide examples of path dependency in the development of specific technologies. Brian Arthur (1989) has suggested a theoretical treatment that falls into the neoclassical/ institutionalist hybrid category.

18. Chester Barnard (1938) may have been the first to propound this view of organization. He coined the phrase 'collective rationality'. Simon (1957) uses and develops this idea.

19. This and subsequent sections draw heavily on Chandler 1977 and 1990. See the very insightful reviews of the latter monumental work, by Teece (1993) and Langlois (1991). Moss (1981) attempts to apply certain concepts that play a role in Chandler's analysis, such as minimum efficient scale.

20. Organizational capabilities probably belong to a broader category that sociologist James Coleman calls 'social capital' (1988: S98). According to Coleman, social capital, like human or physical capital, facilitates certain actions of actors, thereby 'making possible the achievement of certain ends that in its absence would not be possible' (ibid.). The actors can be 'persons or corporate actors', but Coleman's application is limited to persons. He does not mention organizational capabilities, but 'corporate social capital' may be another term to describe these.

21. Prahalad and Hamel identify three characteristics, but one of these, that the capabilities make a contribution to perceived customer satisfaction from the product, is not a sufficient condition, since it also applies to public knowledge used by the firm.

22. Edith Penrose (1959) reported similar findings and developed related concepts before the publication of Chandler's *Strategy and Structure* (1961). In particular, she argued out that firms grow by applying their technical and managerial 'excess capacity' to new areas.

23. See the Appendix to this chapter for an illustration of the concept.

24. Such procedures have been discussed, with differences in emphasis, by a number of authors who use different terms for the phenomenon. What Nelson and Winter (1982) call 'lower order routine' is called 'short-cut' by Gordon (1945), 'programmed behavior' by Simon (1982: vol. 2, 380) and March and Simon (1958), and 'habitual behavior' by Katona (1980).

25. Winter (1986, 1988) uses the terms subordinate and superordinate for lower and higher-order routines.

26. For 'conservatism' in this context, see Kuran (1988).

27. The point is from March and Simon (1958). In their terms, programmed activities drive out non-programmed activities (85). Rosenberg (1976: 125, n.60) expresses the idea as a counterpart to Keynes' oft-quoted quip: 'In the short run we are all preoccupied.' The conservatism generated by routines may also have its own long-run implication: 'In the long run we fall behind.' (Rosenberg does not draw this implication.) This question is discussed in later sections.

28. This point is made by Nelson and Winter (1982). In Berger and Luckman's (1967) terminology routines become 'opaque'.

29. Leijonhufvud (1986) is an interesting treatment of complementarities between inputs.

30. The definition is similar to the one used in Scott (1989), discussed in the previous chapter. This definition has the advantage of covering innovations

made by user firms, who are a significant source of innovation in some industries, as Von Hippel (1988) has shown.

31. The graph is from Gomulka's (1990) treatment of Nelson and Winter (1982). The concepts 'distance' and 'local search' are discussed in the abstract by Nelson and Winter. Empirical application is needed to make these concepts more concrete..

32. Changes in 'technological trajectories' are discussed later.

33. This is uncertainty about production rather than 'competitive' uncertainty about the environment (Lazonick 1990). See next section.

34. The schedule in Figure 5.1 is a convenient way of illustrating the positive relationship between the 'distance' of a project from the firm's capabilities and the hurdle rate it is expected to satisfy. But there is no reason for the relationship to be linear and continuous.

35. Using Scott's (1989) metaphor, $A'B'$ cuts a piece off the 'cake' of satisfactory projects. See the previous chapter.

36. The analogy with Scott's set of investment opportunities breaks down here; he assumes the aggregate set is renewed every period so as to remain constant. This assumption makes the steady-state equilibrium possible. Unlike Scott's 'cake', AB does not show economy-wide investment opportunities. However, even if it did, there is no presumption that it will remain constant through time.

37. Schumpeter uses the term, 'adaptive response' as the opposite of innovative behavior (Schumpeter 1991: 411). Lazonick follows Schumpeter in distinguishing adaptive and innovative strategies. However, the term 'adaptive' is used in the opposite sense by North, who follows Hayek. That is, Hayek and North use 'adaptive' to mean innovative (or 'creative' in Schumpeter's words). Given the terminological chaos, I will stick to 'static' versus 'innovative' as the most obvious terms.

38. Considering focusing devices from a more narrowly technological point of view, 'A fruitful research program would be to examine various technical bottlenecks and classify them according to the costs involved in solving them by reallocating resources as opposed to the possibilities of searching for a technical solution' (Mokyr 1985: 49).

39. This type of strategy is discussed in the next section and in the appendix to this chapter.

40. See Teece 1993 for a discussion and more references for questions about the capabilities approach to the firm and diversification strategies. Chandler argues that the late 1960s wave of corporate acquisitions in the United States led to a breakdown of managerial effectiveness because the businesses acquired were not related to the corporations' capabilities (Chandler 1990 and 1990 introduction to Chandler 1961).

41. Lazonick (1992) suggests that the power of the financial sector worked to the detriment of industry in late nineteenth to early twentieth-century Britain.

42. For an incisive analysis of the issues involved in the biological metaphor see the review of Nelson and Winter (1982) by Mirowski (1988). The use Mokyr makes of evolutionary terminology is suggestive, but prior to using it he makes the same points without the biological analogy. It is not clear that the latter adds any insights to his far-reaching study of technical change.

43. For example, there is disagreement on whether organisms or genes struggle for survival. See Gould 1992.

44. For a detailed discussion of these differences, see Nelson and Winter (1982), especially chapter 6. Also see Langlois (1986 a, b). The selection argument used, for example, by Milton Friedman in his methodological essay seems to be based on crude Darwinian reasoning that is controversial among today's evolutionary biologists. See Gould 1992 for a critique of biological 'survival of the fittest' arguments.

45. Hollander 1965 made this point about Du Pont rayon plants. See Rosenberg 1976 for a general analysis of the cumulative nature of technical change.

46. Mokyr (1990) gives several historical examples of this phenomenon, the most dramatic of which is perhaps the great inventions made in China, which had little economic effect. Incremental improvements and practical applications did not follow the inventions.

47. The different location of the new unit cannot be explained in terms of wage differences because the company potentially could have won further concessions from the union by locating the factory in Michigan.

48. The term 'topography' is used to describe the conditions under which the search takes place, such as at what point a certain possibility can be discerned as information accumulates. These conditions are part of the selection environment that determinesd the success of a firm's search routines.

49. Examples include Amsden (1989), as well as other studies of technical change cited in this chapter.

50. This interpretation of late nineteenth and early twentieth-century British history can be found in Chandler 1990; Mowery and Rosenberg 1989 ch. 5; Lazonick 1990. For the other side of the debate, see McCloskey 1981.

51. Baumol, Blackman and Wolff (1989) is an example of this view.

52. As Teece (1993: 218) points out, Chandler does not distinguish the success of firms from the success of the nation state. In particular, the link between multinational firms and the national economy they originated from requires more study.

53. This characteristic would seem to be common to most 'social capital', as defined by Coleman (1988).

54. See Noble's (1977) account of engineering education and professionalization in the US, and Lazonick (1992: ch. 8) on the historical differences between US and British managerial education.

55. David (1985), in his classic analysis of the QWERTY keyboard, explains path dependency in terms of quasi-irreversibility, complementarity and increasing returns.

56. Of course, if there is a constituency in favor of changing a practice, public agencies may intervene.

57. The industries studied include automobiles, chemicals, aircraft, consumer electronics, machine tools, semiconductors, computers and copiers, steel, textiles (Dertouzos et al. 1989).

58. Cardwell (1972: 210) pointed out that 'no nation has been (technologically) creative for more than a historically short period'; Mokyr (1990: 207) considers this 'Cardwell's Law' a crude empirical generalization. He does not connect it to the capabilities theory of the firm.

59. Olson's (1982) analysis of the rigidity due to entrenched interest groups in the political sphere and North's (1990a) analysis of public institutions

complement this picture. See also Kuran (1988) on the general 'conservatism' caused by institutions.

60.   Price competition in the patent drug market may be incompatible with product competition for several reasons. Demand for patented drugs is price inelastic and there is little incentive for innovating companies to cut prices (Schwartzman 1976: 5). Furthermore, the continuous stream of new products prevents the standardization which could open the way to price competition (Comanor 1986: 1186).

61.   This distinction between patented and generic drug markets is clear-cut for the US, but may be fuzzy in other countries. For example, the Canadian government has a system of 'compulsory licensing' under which drugs still under patent protection are licensed to non-research companies and are subject to price competition like generics (Gorecki 1986). It should be noted that research-based firms compete in terms of quality differences when faced with cheap generic substitutes for their products.

62.   See the 'discussion' of Caves et al. 1991.

63.   The development of a successful product takes 10–12 years on average. Much of the information in this section comes from Wiggins 1981, whose analysis is based on his survey of executives from the 12 major research-oriented drug companies.

64.   This is the process described by Lazonick (1990) for innovative industries in general.

65.   Various developments that have affected the industry are surveyed in Comanor 1986.

66.   Also see James 1977: 74–6.

67.   Orsenigo 1989 is a study of the biotechnology industry from an evolutionary perspective. The book compares the evolution of biotechnology in major industrial countries.

CHAPTER 6: SUMMING UP

1.   The contrast is probably rooted in differences in philosophical foundations. See Mirowski 1988: ch. 7.

2.   Institutions, routines, behavioral norms, etc., are necessarily specific to time and place. This does not rule out formal modeling; it merely means that the models will be history-specific.

3.   To go back to Adam Smith's institutionalist explanation of economic stagnation in China: Why didn't potential investors try to limit the arbitrary appropriations of the mandarins? Because they had the same model of the world as the mandarins, and within this framework such appropriations were a routine occurrence. The mandarins' plunder was not challenged because it was in effect accepted as a social norm, one that had lasted for many centuries.

Bibliography

Abbot, Andrew. 1990. 'Comment: Stinchcombe's "Reason and Rationality"', in *The Limits of Rationality*, M.S. Cook and M. Levi (eds), Chicago and London: University of Chicago Press.

Abramovitz, Moses. 1989. *Thinking About Growth and Other Essays on Economic Growth and Welfare*, Cambridge: Cambridge University Press.

Abramovitz, M. and David, P.A. 1973. 'Reinterpreting American Economic Growth: Parables and Realities', *American Economic Review*, vol. LXIII, no. 2, May.

Allen, G.C. 1981. *The Japanese Economy*, New York: St. Martin's Press.

Amsden, Alice H. 1989. *Asia's Next Giant. South Korea and Late Industrialization*, New York and Oxford: Oxford University Press.

Arora, Ashish and Gambardella, Alfonso. 1990. 'Complementarity and External Linkages: The Strategies of the Large Firms in Biotechnology', *Journal of Industrial Economics*, vol. XXXVIII, no. 4, June.

Arrow, Kenneth J. 1987. 'Rationality of Self and Others in an Economic System' in *Rational Choice. The Contrast Between Economics and Psychology*, R. Hogarth and M. Reder (eds), Chicago and London: Chicago University Press.

____. 1982. 'Risk Perception in Psychology and Economics', *Economic Inquiry*, 20(1).

____. 1974. *The Limits of Organization*, New York: Norton.

____. 1962. 'The Economic Implications of Learning by Doing', *Review of Economic Studies*, vol. 29, June.

Arthur, Brian W. 1989. 'Competing Technologies, Increasing Returns, and Lock-In by Historical Events', *Economic Journal*, 99, March.

____. 1988. 'Competing Technologies: An Overview', in *Technical Change and Economic Theory*, G. Dosi et al. (eds), London: Pinter Publishers.

Asimakopulos, Athanasios. 1990. 'Keynes and Sraffa: Visions and Perspectives' in *Essays on Piero Sraffa*, K. Bharadwaj and B. Schefold, (eds), London: Unwin Hyman.

____. 1977. 'Post-Keynesian Growth Theory' in *Modern Economic Thought*, S. Weintraub (ed.), Philadelphia: University of Pennsylvania.

____. 1971. 'The Determination of Investment in Keynes's Model' in *Canadian Journal of Economics*, IV, 3, August.

Bailey, Martin N. 1972. 'Research and Development Costs and Returns: The U.S. Pharmaceutical Industry', *Journal of Political Economy*, vol. 80, Jan/Feb.

Bairre, James G. 1977. *The Future of the Multinational Pharmaceutical Industry to 1990*, New York and Toronto: Wiley.

Barnard, Chester. 1938. *The Functions of the Executive*, Cambridge, Mass.: Harvard University Press.

Baumol, William; Blackman, S.A. Batey; Wolff, Edward N. 1989. *Productivity and American Leadership. The Long View*, Cambridge, Mass. and London: MIT Press.

Berger, Peter L. and Luckman, Thomas. 1967. *The Social Construction of Reality*, Garden City: Doubleday.

143

Best, Michael. 1990. *The New Competition: Institutions of Industrial Restructuring*, Cambridge, Mass.: Harvard University Press.

Bharadwaj, Krishna. 1986. *Classical Political Economy and Rise to Dominance of Supply and Demand Theories*, London: Sangam Books.

Biddle, Jeff E. 1990. 'The Role of Negotiational Psychology in J.R. Commons's Proposed Reconstruction of Political Economy', *Review of Political Economy*, vol. 2, no. 1.

Blaug, Mark. 1985. *Economic Theory in Retrospect*, fourth edition, Cambridge: Cambridge University Press.

_____. 1963. 'A Survey of Process-Innovations', *Economica*, February.

Bleaney, Michael. 1976. *Underconsumption Theories. A History and Critical Analysis*, New York: International Publishers.

Boskin, Michael J. 1988. 'Tax Policy and Economic Growth: Lessons from the 1980s', *Journal of Economic Perspectives*, vol. 2, Fall.

_____. 1986. 'Macroeconomics, Technology, and Economic Growth: An Introduction to Some Important Issues', in *The Positive Sum Strategy. Harnessing Technology for Economic Growth*, R. Landau and N. Rosenberg, Washington, DC: National Academy Press.

Bosworth, Barry. 1982. 'Capital Formation and Economic Policy', *Brookings Papers on Economic Activity*, 2. Washington DC: Brookings Institution.

Bray, Margaret and Kreps, David M. 1987. 'Rational Learning and Rational Expectations' in *Arrow and the Ascent of Modern Economic Theory*, G. Feiwel (ed.), New York: New York University Press.

Bromiley, Philip. 1986 'Corporate Planning and Capital Investment', *Journal of Economic Behavior and Organization*, vol. 7.

Burmeister, Edwin and Dobell, Rodney A. 1970. *Mathematical Theories of Economic Growth*, New York: Macmillan/London: Collier-Macmillan.

Canterbery, Ray E. 1992. 'An Evolutionary Model of Technical Change with Markup Pricing' in Milberg (ed.), *The Megacorp and Macrodynamics, Essays in Memory of Alfred Eichner*, Armonk, NY: M.E. Sharpe.

Cardwell, D.S.L. 1972. *Turning Points in Western Technology*, New York: Neale Watson Science History Publication.

Caves, Richard E., Whinston, Michael D., Hurwitz, Mark E. 1991. 'Patent Expiration, Entry, and Competition in the U.S. Pharmaceutical Industry', *Brookings Papers on Economic Activity: Microeconomics*. Washington DC: Brookings Institution.

Chandler, Alfred D. Jr. 1992. 'Organizational Capabilities and the Economic History of the Industrial Enterprise', *Journal of Economic Perspectives*, vol. 6, no. 3, Summer.

_____. 1990. *Scale and Scope. The Dynamics of Industrial Capitalism*. Cambridge, Mass.: Belknap Press of Harvard University Press.

_____.1981. 'The American System and Modern Management' in *Yankee Enterprise. The Rise of the American System of Manufactures*, Mayr, O. and Post, R.C. (eds), Washington, DC: Smithsonian Institution Press.

_____. 1977. *The Visible Hand. The Managerial Revolution in American Business*, Cambridge, Mass.: Belknap Press of Harvard University Press.

_____. 1961. *Strategy and Structure. Chapters in the History of the Industrial Enterprise*. Reprinted in 1990 with a new introduction, Cambridge, Mass.: MIT Press.

Ciccone, Roberto. 'Accumulation and Capacity Utilization: Some Critical Considerations on Joan Robinson's Theory of Distribution' in *Essays on Piero Sraffa*, K. Bharadwaj and B. Schefold, (eds), London: Unwin Hyman.

Clark, K.P. 1979. 'Investment in the 1970s: Theory, Performance, and Prediction', *Brookings Papers on Economic Activity*, no. 1. Washington DC: Brookings Institution.

Coen, Robert and Eisner, Robert. 1987. 'Investment' in *The New Palgrave, A Dictionary of Economics*, J. Eatwell, M. Milgate and P. Newman (eds), London: Macmillan.

Coleman, James S. 1990. 'Norm-Generating Structures', in *The Limits of Rationality*, M.S. Cook and M. Levi (eds), Chicago and London: University of Chicago Press.

____. 1988. 'Social Capital in the Creation of Human Capital', *American Journal of Sociology*, vol. 94, supplement S95–120.

Coleman, J.S., Katz, E., Menzel, H. 1966. *Medical Innovation: A Diffusion Study*, Indianapolis: Bobbs-Merrill.

Comanor, William S. 1986. 'The Political Economy of the Pharmaceutical Industry', *Journal of Economic Literature*, vol. XXIV, no. 3, September.

Commons, John R. 1934. *Institutional Economics*, New York: Macmillan.

____. 1924. *Legal Foundations of Capitalism*, New York: Macmillan.

Costabile, Lilia and Rowthorn, Bob. 1985. 'Malthus's Theory of Wages and Growth', *Economic Journal*, June.

Cowan, Robin. 1991. 'Tortoises and Hares: Choice Among Technologies of Unknown Merit', *Economic Journal*, July, 101.

____. 1990. 'Nuclear Power Reactors: A Study in Technological Lock-in', *Journal of Economic History*, September, vol. L, no. 3.

Cyert, Richard M. and March, James G. 1963. *A Behavioral Theory of the Firm*, Englewood Cliffs, NJ: Prentice-Hall.

Dasgupta, Partha and David, Paul A. 1987. 'Information Disclosure and the Economics of Science and Technology' in *Arrow and the Ascent of Modern Economic Theory*, G. Feiwel (ed.), New York: New York University Press.

David, Paul A. 1989. 'Computer and Dynamo: The Modern Productivity Paradox in a Not-Too-Distant Mirror', Center for Economic Policy Research Publication 172, Stanford University Press.

____. 1986. 'Technology Diffusion, Public Policy, and Industrial Competitiveness' in *The Positive Sum Strategy. Harnessing Technology for Economic Growth*, R. Landau and N. Rosenberg, Washington, DC: National Academy Press.

____. 1985. 'Clio and the Economics of QWERTY', *American Economic Review, Papers and Proceedings*, vol. 75, no. 2, May.

____. 1977. 'Invention and Accumulation in America's Economic Growth: A Nineteenth Century Parable' in *International Organization, National Policies and Economic Development*, K. Brunner and A. Meltzer (eds), Amsterdam: North-Holland.

____. 1975. *Technical Choice, Innovation, and Economic Growth: Essays on American and British Experience in the Nineteenth Century*, Cambridge and New York: Cambridge University Press.

Denison, Edward F. 1985. *Trends in American Economic Growth 1929–1982*, Washington, DC: Brookings Institution.

____. 1977. 'A Comment on the North and David Papers' in *International Organization, National Policies and Economic Development*, K. Brunner and A. Meltzer (eds), Amsterdam: North-Holland.

____. 1962. *The Sources of Economic Growth in the United States*, New York: Committee for Economic Development.

Dertouzos, Michael L, et al. 1989. *Made in America. Regaining the Productive Edge*, Cambridge, Mass.: MIT Press.

Duesenberry, J.S. 1958. *Business Cycles and Economic Growth*, New York: McGraw-Hill.

Dugger, William. 1991. *Underground Economics. A Decade of Institutionalist Dissent*, Armonk, NY: M.E. Sharpe.

Dorfman, Joseph. 1934. *Thorstein Veblen and his America*, seventh edition, reprint 1972, Clifton, NJ: Augustus M. Kelley.

Dornbusch, Rudiger, and Fischer, Stanley. 1990. *Macroeconomics*, fifth edition, New York: McGraw-Hill.

Dosi, Giovanni. 1988a. 'Institutions and Markets in a Dynamic World', *The Manchester School*, vol. LVI, June.

____. 1988b. 'Sources, Procedures, and Microeconomic Effects of Innovation', *Journal of Economic Literature*, vol. XXVI, September.

____. 1986. 'Technology and Conditions of Macroeconomic Development' in *Design, Innovation, and Long Cycles in Economic Development*, C. Freeman (ed.), London: Frances Pinter.

____. 1982. 'Technological Paradigms and Technological Trajectories. A Suggested Interpretation of the Determinants and Directions of Technical Change', *Research Policy*, vol. 11, June.

Dosi, Giovanni and Orsenigo, Luigi. 1988. 'Coordination and Transformation. An Overview of Structures, Behaviors and Change in Evolutionary Environments', in *Technical Change and Economic Theory*, G. Dosi et al. (ed), London: Printer Publishers.

Eatwell, John and Milgate, Murray (eds) 1983. *Keynes's Economics and the Theory of Value and Distribution*, New York: Oxford University Press.

Eckaus, Richard. 1969. 'The Acceleration Principle Reconsidered', *Macroeconomic Theory: Selected Readings*, H. Williams and J. Huffnagle (eds), Englewood Cliffs, NJ: Prentice-Hall.

Eichner, Alfred. 1991. *The Macrodynamics of Advanced Market Economies*, Armonk, NY: M.E. Sharpe.

____. 1980. 'A General Model of Investment and Pricing' in *Growth, Profits and Property*, E. Nell (ed.), Cambridge: Cambridge University Press.

____. 1976. *The Megacorp and Oligopoly: Micro Foundations of Macro Dynamics*, Cambridge: Cambridge University Press.

Eisner, Robert. 1985. 'The Total Incomes System of Accounts', *Survey of Current Business*, 65, January.

____. 1978. *Factors in Business Investment*, Cambridge, Mass.: Ballinger.

____. 1956. *Determinants of Capital Expenditures. An Interview Study*, Urbana: University of Illinois Press.

Elbaum, Bernard, and Lazonick, William (eds) 1986. *The Decline of the British Economy*, Oxford: Clarendon Press.

Elster, Jon. 1990. 'When Rationality Fails' in *The Limits of Rationality*, M.S. Cook and M. Levi (eds), Chicago and London: University of Chicago Press.

____. 1989. *Solomonic Judgements*, Cambridge: Cambridge University Press.

Eltis, W.A. 1984. *The Classical Theory of Economic Growth*, New York: St. Martin's Press.

Feiwel, George R. (ed.) 1989. *Joan Robinson and Modern Economic Theory*, New York: New York University Press.

Feldstein, Martin and Horioka, Charles. 1980. 'Domestic Saving and International Capital Flows', *Economic Journal*, vol. 90, June.

Fischer, Stanley. 1988. 'Symposium on the Slowdown in Productivity Growth', *Journal of Economic Perspectives*, Fall.

Fransman, Martin. 1985. 'Conceptualising Technical Change in the Third World in the 1980s: An Interpretive Survey', *Journal of Development Studies*, vol. 21, no. 4.

Freeman, Christopher. 1989. 'The Nature of Innovation and the Evolution of the Productive System', Paris, OECD International Seminar on Science, Technology, and Economic Growth.

____. 1986. *The Economics of Innovation*, second edition, Cambridge, Mass.: MIT Press.

Freeman, Christopher and Perez, Carlota. 1988. 'Structural Crises of Adjustment: Business Cycles and Investment Behavior', in *Technical Change and Economic Theory*, G. Dosi et al. (eds), London: Pinter Publishers.

Garegnani, Pierangelo. 1992. 'Some Notes for an Analysis of Accumulation' in *Beyond the Steady State. A Revival of Growth Theory*, J. Halevi, D. Laibman, E. Nell (eds), London: Macmillan.

____. 1987. 'Capital and Effective Demand' in *Keynes Today*, A. Barriere (ed.), London: Macmillan.

____. 1984. 'Value and Distribution in the Classical Economists and Marx', *Oxford Economic Papers*, 36, 291–325.

____. 1983. 'Notes on Consumption, Investment and Effective Demand' in J. Eatwell and M. Milgate (eds), *Keynes's Economics and the Theory of Value and Distribution*, New York: Oxford University Press.

____. 1976. 'On a Change in the Notion of Equilibrium in Recent Work on Value and Distribution', *Essays in Modern Capital Theory*, M. Brown, K. Sato, P. Zarembka (eds), Amsterdam: North-Holland.

Gilad, Benjamin and Kaish, Stanley. 1986. *Handbook of Behavioral Economics*, vol. A, Behavioral Microeconomics, Greenwich, Conn.: JAI Press.

Gomulka, Stanislaw. 1990. *The Theory of Technological Change and Economic Growth*, London and New York: Routledge.

Gordon, D.M. 1991. 'Kaldor's Macro System: Too Much Cumulation, Too Few Contradictions' in Edward Nell and Willi Semmler (eds), *Nicholas Kaldor and Mainstream Economics, Confrontation or Convergence*? New York: St. Martin's Press.

Gordon, David, Wiesskopf, Thomas and Bowles, Samuel. 1986. 'Power and Profits: The Social Structure of Accumulation and the Profitability of the Postwar U.S. Economy' in *Review of Radical Political Economics*, vol. 18, Spring and Summer.

Gordon, Robert A. 1945. *Business Leadership in the Large Corporation*. Washington, DC: Brookings Institution.

Gorecki, Paul K. 1986. 'The Importance of Being First', *International Journal of Industrial Organization*, vol. 4, December.

Gould, Stephen Jay. 1992. 'The Confusion over Evolution', *New York Review of Books*, 19 November.

Grabowski, Henry G. 1991. 'Changing Economics of Pharmaceutical R&D', in *The Changing Economics of Medical Technology*, vol. II, *Medical Innovation at the Crossroads*, Washington, DC: National Academy Press.

____. 1989. 'An Analysis of U.S. International Competitiveness in Pharmaceuticals', *Managerial and Decision Economics*, Special Issue, Spring.

Grabowski, Henry and Vernon, John. 1981. 'The Determinants of Research and Development Expenditures in the Pharmaceutical Industry' in *Drugs and Health. Economic Issues and Policy Objectives*, R. Helms (ed.), Washington DC: American Enterprise Institute.

Griliches, Zvi. 1990. 'Patent Statistics as Economic Indicators: A Survey', *Journal of Economic Literature*, vol. XXVIII, no. 4, December.

____. 1988. 'Productivity Puzzles and R&D: Another Nonexplanation', *Journal of Economic Perspectives*, vol. 2, Fall.

____. (ed.) 1987. *R&D, Patents, and Productivity*, Chicago: Chicago University Press.

Haavelmo, T. 1960. *A Study in the Theory of Investment*, Chicago: University of Chicago Press.

Hahn, F.H. and Matthews, R.C.O. 1964. 'The Theory of Economic Growth: A Survey', *Economic Journal*, vol. 74.

Halevi, Joseph, Laibman, David and Nell, Edward. 1992. *Beyond the Steady State. A Revival of Growth Theory*, London: Macmillan.

Hansen, Alvin H. 1964. Business Cycles and National Income, expanded edn, New York: Norton.

Harcourt, G.C. 1982. *The Social Science Imperialists*, London: Routledge & Kegan Paul.

Harris, Donald. 1978. *Capital Accumulation and Income Distribution*, Stanford: Stanford University Press.

Hayes, Robert H. and Abernathy, William J .1980. 'Managing Our Way to Economic Decline', *Harvard Business Review*, vol. 58, July–August.

Heilbroner, Robert L. 1985. *The Nature and Logic of Capitalism*, New York: Norton.

____. 1980. *Marxism: For and Against*, New York and London: Norton.

Hilts, Philip J. 1992. 'Plan to Speed Approval of Drugs: Makers Would Pay Fees to the U.S.', *New York Times*, 8 November.

Hirshleifer, Jack and Riley, John G. 1992. *The Analytics of Uncertainty and Information*. Cambridge: Cambridge University Press.

Hodgson, Geoffrey M. 1988. *Economics and Institutions. A Manifesto for a Modern Institutional Economics*, Philadelphia: University of Pennsylvania Press.

Hollander, Samuel. 1979. *The Economics of David Ricardo*, Toronto: University of Toronto Press.

____. 1973. *The Economics of Adam Smith*, Toronto: University of Toronto Press.

____. 1965. *The Sources of Increased Efficiency: A Study of Du Pont Rayon Plants*, Cambridge, Mass.: MIT Press.

James, Barrie. 1977. *The Future of the Multinational Pharmaceutical Industry to 1990*, New York, Toronto: John Wiley.

Johnson, Thomas and Kaplan, Robert. 1987. *Relevance Lost: The Rise and Fall of Management Accounting*, Cambridge: Harvard Business School Press.

Jones, Hywel G. 1976. *An Introduction to Modern Theories of Economic Growth*, New York: McGraw-Hill.

Jorgenson, Dale W. 1989. 'Capital as a Factor of Production', *Technology and Capital Formation*, D.W. Jorgenson and R. Landau (eds), Cambridge, Mass.: MIT Press.

____. 1969. 'The Theory of Investment Behavior' *Macroeconomic Theory: Selected Readings*, H. Williams and J. Huffnagle (eds), Englewood Cliffs, NJ: Prentice-Hall.

____. 1963. 'Capital Theory and Investment Behavior', *American Economic Review*, 53.

Kaldor, Nicholas. 1985. *Economics Without Equilibrium*, Armonk, NY: M.E. Sharpe.

____. 1970 Model of Distribution in A. Sen (ed.), *Growth Economics*, Harmondsworth, Middlesex: Penguin.

____. 1967. *Strategic Factors in Economic Development*, Ithaca, NY: Cornell University, Press.

____. 1961. 'Capital Accumulation and Economic Growth', in *The Theory of Capital*, Lutz F.A. and Hague D.C. (eds), London: Macmillan.

____. 1957. 'A Model of Economic Growth', *Economic Journal*, vol. 67, December.

____. 1954. 'The Relation of Economic Growth and Cyclical Fluctuations', *Economic Journal*, vol. 64, March.

____. 1951. 'Mr. Hicks on the Trade Cycle', *Economic Journal*, vol. 61, December.

Kaldor, N. and Mirrless, J. 1962. 'A New Model of Economic Growth', *Review of Economic Studies*, vol. XXIX, no. 3.

Kalecki, Michal. 1971. *Selected Essays of the Dynamics of the Capitalist Economy 1933–1970*, Cambridge: Cambridge University Press.

____. 1969. *Theory of Economic Dynamics. An Essay on Cyclical and Long-Run Changes in Capitalist Economies*, New York: A. Kelley.

Kamien, Morton I. and Schwartz, Nancy L. 1982. *Market Structure and Innovation*, Cambridge: Cambridge University Press.

Katona, George. 1980. *Essays on Behavioral Economics*, Ann Arbor, Mich.: Institute for Social Research, University of Michigan.

Keynes, John Maynard. 1987. *The Collected Writings of John Maynard Keynes*, vols. XIII and XIV; *The General Theory and After*, London and Cambridge: Macmillan and Cambridge University Press for the Royal Economic Society, paperback edition.

____. 1971. *The Treatise on Money*, London: Macmillan.

____. 1964. *The General Theory of Employment, Interest and Money*, New York and London: Harcourt Brace Jovanovich. Originally published 1936.

Klein, Lawrence R. 1958. 'Review of The Accumulation of Capital', *Econometrica*, vol. XXVI.

Kline, Stephen J. and Rosenberg, Nathan. 1986. 'An Overview of Innovation', in *The Positive Sum Strategy. Harnessing Technology for Economic Growth*, R. Landau and N. Rosenberg, Washington, DC: National Academy Press.

Knight, Frank H. 1971. *Risk, Uncertainty and Profit*, Chicago: University of Chicago Press.

Kregel, J.A. 1975. *The Reconstruction of Political Economy. An Introduction to Post-Keynesian Economics*, London: Macmillan.

Kuran, Timur. 1988. 'The Tenacious Past: Theories of Personal and Collective Conservatism', *Journal of Economic Behavior and Organization*, 10.

Kurdas, Chidem. 1993. 'Classical Perspectives on Investment: An Exegesis of Behavioral Assumptions' in *Economics as Worldly Philosophy. Essays in Political and Historical Economics in Honour of Robert L. Heilbroner*, New York: St. Martin's Press.

_____. 1992. 'Technological Competition and the Determinants of Investment Spending' in *Macroeconomic Theory: Diversity and Convergence*, G. Mongiovi and C. Ruhl (eds), Cheltenham, Glos. and Brookfield, Vermont: Edward Elgar.

_____. 1991. 'Robinson's Dark Room: Investment in Post-Keynesian Growth Theory' in *The Joan Robinson Legacy*, I. Rima (ed.), Armonk, NY : M.E. Sharpe.

_____. 1988. 'The Whig Historian on Adam Smith: Paul Samuelson's Canonical Classical Model', *History of Economics Society Bulletin* (*Journal of the History of Economic Thought*), Spring, 10(1).

Kurz, H.D. 1991. 'Technical Change, Growth and Distribution: A Steady-State Approach to 'Unsteady' Growth on Kaldorian Lines' in Edward Nell and Willi Semmler (eds), *Nicholas Kaldor and Mainstream Economics, Confrontation or Convergence?* New York: St. Martin's Press.

_____. 1990. 'Accumulation, Distribution and the "Keynesian Hypothesis"' in *Essays on Piero Sraffa*, K. Bharadwaj and B. Schefold, (eds), London: Unwin Hyman.

Kuznets, Simon. 1966. *Modern Economic Growth: Rate, Structure and Spread*, New Haven and London: Yale University Press.

Laibman, David. 1992a. 'Immanent Critical Tendencies: Toward A Comprehensive Theory', Brooklyn College of the City University of New York.

_____. 1992b. *Value, Technical Change, and Crisis. Explorations in Marxist Economic Theory*. Armonk, NY: M.E. Sharpe.

_____. 1987. 'Technical Change and the Contradictions of Capitalism' in *The Imperiled Economy*, Cherry et al. (eds), New York: URPE.

_____. 1983. 'Capitalism and Immanent Crisis: Broad Strokes for a Theoretical Foundation', *Social Research*, vol. 50, Summer.

Landau, Ralph. 1989. 'Technology and Capital Formation', *Technology and Capital Formation*, D.W. Jorgenson and R. Landau (eds), Cambridge, Mass.: MIT Press.

Landau, Ralph, and Hotsopoulos, George. 1986. 'Capital Formation in the United States and Japan', in *The Positive Sum Strategy. Harnessing Technology for Economic Growth*, R. Landau and N. Rosenberg, Washington, DC: National Academy Press.

Landes, David S. *The Unbound Prometheus. Technological Change and Industrial Development in Western Europe from 1750 to the Present*. Cambridge: Cambridge University Press.

Langlois, Richard N. 1992. 'The Capabilities of Industrial Capitalism', *Critical Review*, vol. 5: 4, Fall.

_____. 1989. 'What was Wrong with the Old Institutional Economics (and What is still Wrong with the New)?', *Review of Political Economy*, vol. 1, no. 3, November.

_____. 1988. 'Economic Change and the Boundaries of the Firm', *Journal of Institutional and Theoretical Economics*, 144, no. 4, November.

_____. 1986a. 'The New Institutional Economics: An Introductory Essay' in *Economics as a Process: Essays in the New Institutional Economics*, R. Langlois (ed.), Cambridge and New York: Cambridge University Press.

____. 1986b. 'Rationality, Institutions and Explanation' in *Economics as a Process: Essays in the New Institutional Economics*, R. Langlois (ed.), Cambridge and New York: Cambridge University Press.

Lazonick, William. 1992. *Organization and Technology in Capitalist Development*, Cheltenham, Glos. and Brookfield, Vermont: Edward Elgar.

____. 1991. *Business Organization and the Myth of the Market Economy.* Cambridge: Cambridge University Press.

____. 1990. *Competitive Advantage on the Shop Floor.* Cambridge, Mass.: Harvard University Press.

Leijonhufvud, Axel. 1986. 'Capitalism and the Factory System' in *Economics as a Process: Essays in the New Institutional Economics*, R. Langlois (ed.), Cambridge and New York: Cambridge University Press.

Levin, Richard C. et al. 1987. 'Appropriating the Returns from Industrial Research and Development', *Brookings Papers on Economic Activity*, Special Issue on Microeconomics, 3. Washington DC: Brookings Institution.

Levine, David P. 1981. *Economic Theory*, vol. II: *The System of Economic Relations as a Whole*, London, Boston and Henley: Routledge & Kegan Paul.

Lipietz, Alain. 1986. 'Behind the Crisis: The Exhaustion of a Regime of Accumulation. A Regulation School Perspective on Some French Empirical Works', *Review of Radical Political Economy*, Spring and Summer.

Loasby, Brian J. 1991. 'Joan Robinson's "Wrong Turning"' in *The Joan Robinson Legacy*, I. Rima (ed.), Armonk, NY: M.E. Sharpe.

____. 1986. 'Organization, Competition, and the Growth of Knowledge' in *Economics as a Process: Essays in the New Institutional Economics*, R. Langlois (ed.), Cambridge and New York: Cambridge University Press.

Lowe, Adolph. 1976. *The Path of Economic Growth*, Cambridge: Cambridge University Press.

Lucas, Robert E. 1987. 'Adaptive Behavior and Economic Theory' in *Rational Choice. The Contrast Between Economics and Psychology*, R. Hogarth and M. Reder (eds), Chicago and London: Chicago University Press.

Lucas, Robert E. and Prescott, Edward C. 1971. 'Investment under Uncertainty', *Econometrica*, 39(5).

Lund Philip. 1971. *Investment. The Study of an Economic Aggregate*, Amsterdam: North-Holland.

Maddison, Angus. 1991. *Dynamic Forces in Capitalist Development*, Oxford and New York: Oxford University Press.

____. 1987. 'Growth and Slowdown in Advanced Capitalist Economies', *Journal of Economic Literature*, vol. xxv, June.

____. 1982. *Phases of Capitalist Development.* Oxford and New York: Oxford University Press.

Majewski, Raymond. 1988. 'The Hayek Challenge and the Origins of Chapter 17 of Keynes' *General Theory*' in *Keynes's General Theory nach Funfzig Jahren*, H. Hagemann and O. Steiger (eds), Berlin: Duncker & Humblot.

Malthus, Thomas R. 1963. 'Review of Essay on Political Economy', first published in the *Quarterly Review*, 1824, reprinted in *Occasional Papers of T.R. Malthus*, A. Semmel (ed.), New York: Burt Franklin.

____. 1836. *Principles of Political Economy, Considered with a View to Their Practical Application*, 2nd edition, New York: Kelley, 1951.

March, James G. and Simon, Herbert A. 1958. *Organizations.* New York: Wiley.

Marglin, Stephen A. 1987. 'Investment and Accumulation' in J. Eatwell, M. Milgate and P. Newman (eds), *The New Palgrave, A Dictionary of Economics*, London: Macmillan.

_____. 1984. *Growth, Distribution and Prices*, Cambridge, Mass:Harvard University Press.

Marglin, Stephen A. and Bhaduri, A, 1991. 'Profit Squeeze and Keynesian Theory' in Edward Nell and Willi Semmler (eds), *Nicholas Kaldor and Mainstream Economics, Confrontation or Convergence?* New York: St. Martin's Press.

Marris, Robin. 1964. *The Economic Theory of Managerial Capitalism*, New York: Basic Books.

Marris, Robin and Wood, Adrian. 1971. *The Corporate Economy. Growth, Competition, and Innovative Potential*, Cambridge, Mass: Harvard University Press.

Marx, Karl. 1967. *Capital*, vols. 2 and 3, New York: International Publishers.

_____. 1963. *Early Writings*, translated and edited by T. Bottomore, New York: McGraw-Hill.

_____. 1954. *Capital. A Critical Analysis of Capitalist Production*, vol. 1, Moscow: Progress Publishers.

McCloskey, Donald N. 1981. *Enterprise and Trade in Victorian Britain: Essays in Historical Economics*, London: Allen & Unwin.

Milberg, William. 1992. 'Introduction: Social Thought and Social Change – Alfred Eichner's Vision of a New Economics' in Milberg (ed.), *The Megacorp and Macrodynamics, Essays in Memory of Alfred Eichner*, Armonk, NY: M.E. Sharpe.

Milberg, William and Elmslie, Bruce. 1992. 'Technical Change in the Corporate Economy: A Vertically Integrated Approach' in W. Milberg (ed.), *The Megacorp and Macrodynamics, Essays in Memory of Alfred Eichner*, Armonk, NY: M.E. Sharpe.

Miller, Gary J. 1990. 'Managerial Dilemmas: Political Leadership in Hierarchies', in *The Limits of Rationality*, M.S. Cook and M. Levi (eds), Chicago and London: University of Chicago Press.

Minsky, Hyman P. 1982. 'Can "It" Happen Again?' *Essays on Instability and Finance*, Armonk, NY: M.E. Sharpe.

_____. 1975. *John Maynard Keynes*, New York: Columbia University Press.

Mirowski, Philip. 1988. *Against Mechanism: Protecting Economics from Science*. Lanham, Md: Rowman & Littlefield.

_____. 1986. 'Introduction: Paradigms, Hard Cores, and Fuglemen in Modern Economic Theory' in *The Reconstruction of Economic Theory*, P. Mirowski (ed.), Boston: Kluwer-Nijhoff.

Mokyr, Joel. 1990. *The Lever of Riches. Technological Creativity and Economic Progress*, Oxford: Oxford University Press.

_____. 1985. 'The Industrial Revolution and the New Economic History', *The Economics of the Industrial Revolution*, J. Mokyr (ed.), Totowa, NJ: Rowman & Allanheld.

Mongiovi, Gary. 1988. 'On the Determinants of Investment' in *Keynes' Theory of Effective Demand and the Classical Theory of Value and Distribution: The Implications of Sraffa for Macroeconomic Analysis*, PhD dissertation, New York: New School for Social Research.

Moss, Scott J. 1981. *An Economic Theory of Business Strategy: An Essay in Dynamics without Equilibrium*, Oxford: Oxford University Press.

Mowery, David C. and Rosenberg, Nathan. 1989. *Technology and the Pursuit of Economic Growth*, Cambridge: Cambridge University Press.

Munkirs, John R. 1985. *The Transformation of American Capitalism: From Competitive Market Structures to Centralized Private Sector Planning*, Armonk, NY: M.E. Sharpe.

Myers, Stewart C. 1984.'Finance Theory and Financial Strategy' *Interfaces*, 14: 126–37.

Nell, Edward J. 1992a. 'Demand, Pricing, and Investment' in Milberg (ed.), *The Megacorp and Macrodynamics, Essays in Memory of Alfred Eichner*, Armonk, NY: M.E. Sharpe.

_____. 1992b. *Transformational Growth and Effective Demand*, New York: New York University Press.

_____. 1989a. 'Accumulation and Capital Theory' in *Joan Robinson and Modern Economic Theory*, G. Feiwel (ed.), New York: New York University Press.

_____. 1989b. 'Steady Prices in an Unsteady World', New York: New School for Social Research.

_____. 1988. *Prosperity and Public Spending. Transformational Growth and the Role of Government*, Winchester, Mass.: Allen & Unwin.

_____. 1987. 'Accumulation of Capital' in *The New Palgrave: A Dictionary of Economics*, J. Eatwell, M. Milgate and P. Newman (eds), London: Macmillan.

Nelson, Richard R. 1991. 'Why Do Firms Differ, and How Does it Matter?' *Strategic Management Journal*, vol. 12, Winter.

_____. 1990. 'The U.S. Technology Lead: Where Did it Come from and Where Did it Go?', *Research Policy*, vol. 19, April.

_____. 1988. 'Modelling Connections in the Cross Section Between Technical Progress and R&D Intensity', *Rand Journal of Economics*, Autumn, vol. 19, no. 3.

_____. 1987. *Understanding Technical Change as an Evolutionary Process*, Amsterdam and New York: North-Holland.

_____. 1986. 'The Tension between Process Stories and Equilibrium Models: Analyzing the Productivity-Growth Slowdown of the 1970s' in *Economics as a Process: Essays in the New Institutional Economics*, R. Langlois (ed.), Cambridge and New York: Cambridge University Press.

_____. 1981. 'Research on Productivity Growth and Productivity Differences: Dead Ends and New Departures', *Journal of Economic Literature*.

_____. 1973.'Recent Exercises in Growth Accounting: New Understanding or Dead End', *American Economic Review*.

Nelson, Richard and Winter, Sidney. 1982. *An Evolutionary Theory of Economic Change*, Cambridge, Mass.: Belknap Press of Harvard University Press.

_____. 1977. 'In Search of a Useful Theory of Innovation', *Research Policy*, vol. 6.

_____. 1973. 'Toward an Evolutionary Theory of Economic Capabilities', *American Economic Review*, vol. 63, May.

Nelson, Richard and Wright, Gavin. 1992. 'The Rise and Fall of American Technological Leadership: The Postwar Era in Historical Perspective', *Journal of Economic Literature*, vol. XXX, December.

Noble, David. 1984. *Forces of Production. A Social History of Industrial Automation*, New York and Oxford: Oxford University Press.

_____. 1977. *America by Design. Science, Technology, and the Rise of Corporate Capitalism*, New York and Oxford: Oxford University Press.

North, Douglass C. 1990a. 'Institutions and Their Consequences for Economic Performance', in *The Limits of Rationality*, M.S. Cook and M. Levi (eds), Chicago and London: University of Chicago Press.

154   *Bibliography*

____. 1990b. *Institutions, Institutional Change and Economic Performance*, Cambridge and New York: Cambridge University Press.

Olson, Mancur. 1982. *The Rise and Decline of Nations*, New Haven: Yale University Press.

Orsenigo, Luigi. 1989. *The Emergence of Biotechnology. Institutions and Markets in Industrial Innovation*, New York: St. Martin's Press.

Parker, William. 1984. *Europe, America, and the Wider World*. Cambridge: Cambridge University Press.

Pasinetti, Luigi. 1981. *Structural Change and Economic Growth. A Theoretical Essay on the Dynamics of the Wealth of Nations*, Cambridge and New York: Cambridge University Press.

____. 1974. *Growth and Income Distribution. Essays in Economic Theory*, Cambridge and New York: Cambridge University Press.

Peach, Terry. 1993. *Interpreting Ricardo*, Cambridge and New York: Cambridge University Press.

Penrose, Edith. 1959. *The Theory of the Growth of the Firm*, Oxford: Basil Blackwell.

Piore, Michael and Sabel, Charles. 1984. *The Second Industrial Divide*, New York: Basic Books.

Prahalad, C.K., and Hamel, Gary, 1990. 'The Core Competence of the Corporation', *Harvard Business Review*, May–June.

Reuben, Bryan G. and Wittcaff, Harold A. 1989. *Pharmaceutical Chemicals in Perspective*, New York: John Wiley.

Ricardo, David. 1951 onwards. *The Works and Correspondence of David Ricardo*, P. Sraffa (ed.), New York and Cambridge: Cambridge University Press.

Robinson, Joan. 1980. *What are the Questions? And Other Essays*, Armonk, New York: M.E. Sharpe.

____. 1974. *History versus Equilibrium*, London: Thames Polytechnic. Thames Papers in Political Economy.

____. 1965. *The Accumulation of Capital*, 2nd edition, New York: St. Martin's Press.

____. 1964. *Essays in the Theory of Growth*, London: Macmillan.

Romer, Paul M. 1990. 'Endogenous Technological Change', *Journal of Political Economy*, vol. 98, no. 5.

____. 1989. 'Capital Accumulation in the Theory of Long-Run Growth' in *Modern Business Cycle Theory*, R.J. Barro (ed.), Cambridge, Mass.: Harvard University Press.

____. 1986. 'Increasing Returns and Long-Run Growth', *Journal of Political Economy*, vol. 94, October.

Rosenberg, Nathan. 1986. 'The Impact of Technological Innovation: A Historical View', in *The Positive Sum Strategy. Harnessing Technology for Economic Growth*, R. Landau and N. Rosenberg, Washington, DC: National Academy Press.

____. 1982. *Inside The Black Box. Technology and Economics*, Cambridge: Cambridge University Press.

____. 1981. 'Why in America?' in *Yankee Enterprise. The Rise of the American System of Manufactures*, Otto Mayr and Robert Post (eds). Washington, DC: Smithsonian Institution Press.

____. 1976. *Perspectives on Technology*, Armonk, NY: M.E. Sharpe.

____. 1972. *Technology and American Economic Growth*. Armonk, NY: M.E. Sharpe.

____. 1960. 'Some Institutional Aspects of the Wealth of Nations', *Journal of Political Economy*, vol. 68, December.

Rosenberg, Nathan and Birdzell, L.E. 1986. *How the West Grew Rich. The Economic Transformation of the Industrial World*, New York: Basic Books.

Rutherford, Malcolm, 1989. 'What is Wrong with the New Institutional Economics (and What is Still Wrong with the Old)?' *Review of Political Economy*, vol. 1, no. 3, November.

Rymes, Thomas K. 1989. 'Technical Progress, Research, and Development' in *Joan Robinson and Modern Economic Theory*, G. Feiwel (ed.), New York: New York University Press.

Salter, E.E.G. 1960. *Productivity and Technical Change*, Cambridge: Cambridge University Press.

Samuelson, Paul A. 1969. 'Interactions between the Multiplier and the Principle of Acceleration' in *Macroeconomic Theory: Selected Readings*, H. Williams and J. Huffnagle (eds), Englewood Cliffs, NJ: Prentice-Hall.

Sato, Kazuo. 1987. 'Saving and Investment', *The Political Economy of Japan*, vol. I, Stanford: Stanford University Press.

Sawyer, Malcolm C. 1985. *The Economics of Michal Kalecki*, Armonk, NY: M.E. Sharpe.

Scherer, F.M. 1992a. 'Schumpeter and Plausible Capitalism', *Journal of Economic Literature*, vol. XXX, no. 3, September.

____. 1992b. *International High-Technology Competition*, Cambridge, Mass.: Harvard University Press.

____. 1984. *Innovation and Growth, Schumpeterian Perspectives*, Cambridge, Mass.: MIT Press.

____. 1981. 'Commentary' in *Drugs and Health. Economic Issues and Policy Objectives*, R. Helms (ed.), Washington DC: American Enterprise Institute.

Schmookler, Jacob. 1966. *Invention and Economic Growth*, Cambridge, Mass.: Harvard University Press.

Schumpeter, Joseph A. 1991. *The Economics and Sociology of Capitalism*, Richard Swedberg, ed., Princeton, NJ: Princeton University Press. Paper first published 1947.

____. 1955. *The Theory of Economic Development. An Inquiry into Profits, Capital, Credit, Interest, and the Business Cycle*, Cambridge, Mass.: Harvard University Press. (First published in English 1934).

____. 1954. *History of Economic Analysis*, Oxford: Oxford University Press.

____. 1950. *Capitalism, Socialism, and Democracy*, New York: Harper & Row.

____. 1947. 'The Creative Response in Economic History', *Journal of Economic History*, vol. VII, no. 2, November. Reprinted in Schumpeter 1991 as part of ch. 10.

Schwartzman, David. 1976. *Innovation in the Pharmaceutical Industry*, Baltimore and London: Johns Hopkins University Press.

____. 1975. *The Expected Return from Pharmaceutical Research*, Washington, DC: American Enterprise Institute.

Scott, Maurice Fitzgerald. 1989. *A New View of Economic Growth*, Oxford: Clarendon Press.

Sen, Amartya. 1970. 'Introduction' in *Growth Economics*, A. Sen (ed.), Harmondsworth: Penguin.

Shackle, G.L.S. 1983. *The Years of High Theory. Invention & Tradition in Economic Thought 1926–1939*, Cambridge: Cambridge University Press.

Shapiro, Nina. 1986. 'Innovation, New Industries, and New Firms', *Eastern Economic Journal*, vol. XII, January–March.

_____. 1981. 'Pricing and the Growth of the Firm' *Journal of Post-Keynesian Economics*, vol. IV, Fall.

Simon, Herbert A. 1991a. 'Organizations and Markets', *Journal of Economic Perspectives*, Spring, vol. 5, no. 2.

_____. 1991b. *Models of My Life*, New York: Basic Books.

_____. 1987. 'Rationality in Psychology and Economics' in *Rational Choice. The Contrast Between Economics and Psychology*, R. Hogarth and M. Reder (eds), Chicago and London: Chicago University Press.

_____. 1984. 'On the Behavioral and Rational Foundations of Economic Dynamics', *Journal of Economic Behavior and Organization*, vol. 5.

_____. 1982. *Models of Bounded Rationality*, vols. 1–2, Cambridge, Mass.: MIT Press.

_____. 1957. *Models of Man. Social and Rational*, New York: John Wiley.

_____. 1947. *Administrative Behavior*, New York: Macmillan.

Skinner, A.S. and Wilson, T. (eds) 1976. *Essays on Adam Smith*, Oxford: Oxford University Press.

Smith, Adam. 1776. *An Inquiry into the Nature and Causes of the Wealth of Nations*, R.H. Campbell and A.S. Skinner (eds), Oxford University Press edition originally published 1976, Indianapolis: Liberty Classics.

Solow, Robert M. 1970. *Growth Theory*, Oxford: Oxford University Press.

Sraffa, Piero. 1960. *Production of Commodities by Means of Commodities*, Cambridge: Cambridge University Press.

Steindl, Josef. 1976. *Maturity and Stagnation in American Capitalism*, New York and London: Monthly Review Press.

Stiglitz, Joseph E. 1987. 'Technological Change, Sunk Costs, and Competition', *Brookings Papers on Economic Activity*, Special Issue on Microeconomics, 3. Washington DC: Brookings Institution.

Sylos-Labini, Paolo. 1984. *The Forces of Economic Growth and Decline*, Cambridge, Mass.: MIT Press.

_____. 1969. *Oligopoly and Technical Change*, Cambridge, Mass.: Harvard University Press.

Teece, David. 1993. 'The Dynamics of Industrial Capitalism: Perspectives on Alfred Chandler's *Scale and Scope*', *Journal of Economic Literature*, 1993, vol. XXXI.

_____. 1988. 'Technological Change and the Nature of the Firm', in *Technical Change and Economic Theory*, G. Dosi et al. (eds), London: Pinter Publishers.

_____. 1986. 'Profiting from Technological Innovation: Implications for Integration, Collaboration, Licensing, and Public Policy', *Research Policy*, 15, December.

_____. 1980. 'Economies of Scope and the Scope of the Enterprise', *Journal of Economic Behavior and Organization*, no. 3.

Telling, Frederick W. 1992. 'Managed Care and Pharmaceutical Innovation" in *The Changing Economics of Medical Technology, vol. III, Technology and Health Care in an Era of Limits*, Washington, DC: National Academy Press.

Temin, Peter. 1981. 'Physician Prescribing Behavior: Is There Learning by Doing?' in *Drugs and Health. Economic Issues and Policy Objectives*, R. Helms (ed.), Washington DC: American Enterprise Institute.

____. 1980. *Taking your Medicine: Drug Regulation in the United States*, Cambridge, Mass.: Harvard University Press.

Tesar, Linda L. 1991. 'Saving, Investment and International Capital Flows', *Journal of International Economics*, vol. 31, August.

Thirlwall, Anthony P. 1987. *Nicholas Kaldor*, New York: New York University Press.

Thomson, Ross. 1989. 'Economic Forms of Technological Change', presented at the Conference on the Process of Technological change held at the New School for Social Research, New York.

____. 1987. 'Learning by Selling and Invention: The Case of the Sawing Machine', *Journal of Economic History*, vol. XLVII.

____. 1986. 'Technological Change as New Product Development', *Social Concept*, vol. 3.

Tucker, Robert C. (ed.). 1978. *The Marx-Engels Reader*, 2nd edition, New York: Norton.

Tversky, Amos, and Kahneman, Daniel. 1990. 'Rational Choice and the Framing of Decisions', in *The Limits of Rationality*, M.S. Cook and M. Levi (eds), Chicago and London: University of Chicago Press.

Veblen, Thorstein. 1948. *The Portable Veblen*. Edited by Max Lerner, New York: Viking Press.

____. 1919. *The Place of Science in Modern Civilization and Other Essays*, New York: Huebsch.

____. 1915. *Imperial Germany and the Industrial Revolution*, New York: Kelley, 1964 reprint.

Vianello, Fernando. 1985. 'The Pace of Accumulation', *Political Economy. Studies in the Surplus Approach*, vol. 1, no. 1.

von Hippel, Eric. 1988. *The Sources of Innovation*. New York and Oxford: Oxford University Press.

Waterson, Michael. 1984. *Economic Theory of the Industry*, New York and Cambridge: Cambridge University Press.

West, E.G. 1982. 'Ricardo in Historical Perspective', *Canadian Journal of Economics*, vol. XIV, May.

Wiggins, Steven N. 1981. 'The Pharmaceutical Research and Development Decision Process' in *Drugs and Health. Economic Issues and Policy Objectives*, R. Helms (ed.), Washington DC: American Enterprise Institute.

Williamson, Jeffrey G. 1991. 'Productivity and American Leadership: A Review Article', *Journal of Economic Literature*, March, vol. XXIX.

Williamson, Oliver E. 1988. 'The Logic of Economic Organization', *Journal of Law, Economics, and Organization*, vol. 4, no. 1, Spring.

____. 1985. *The Economic Institutions of Capitalism*, New York: Free Press.

____. 1971. 'Managerial Discretion, Organization Form, and the Multi-Division Hypothesis' in R. Marris and A. Wood (eds), *The Corporate Economy. Growth, Competition, and Innovative Potential, Cambridge*, Mass.: Harvard University Press.

Winter, Sidney G. 1988. 'On Coase, Competence, and the Corporation', *Journal of Law, Economics, and Organization*, vol. 4, no. 1, Spring.

____. 1987. 'Comments on Arrow and on Lucas' in *Rational Choice. The Contrast Between Economics and Psychology*, R. Hogarth and M. Reder (eds), Chicago and London: Chicago University Press.

____. 1986. 'The Research Program of the Behavioral Theory of the Firm: Orthodox Critique and Evolutionary Perspective' in *Handbook of Behavioral Economics*, vol. A. Behavioral Microeconomics. B. Gilad and S. Kaish (eds), Greenwich, Conn.: JAI Press.

____. 1971. 'Satisficing, Selection and the Innovating Remnant', *Quarterly Journal of Economics*, vol. 18, May.

____. 1964. 'Economic "Natural Selection" and the Theory of the Firm', *Yale Economic Essays*, 4(1).

Wood, Adrian. 1975. *A Theory of Profits*, Cambridge: Cambridge University Press.

____. 1971. 'Economic Analysis of the Corporate Economy' in R. Marris and A. Wood (eds), *The Corporate Economy. Growth, Competition, and Innovative Potential, Cambridge*, Mass.: Harvard University Press.

Index

159